Discard okay!

The Land Divided,
The World United

On August 15, 1914, a dream, centuries old, came true when the United States opened the Panama Canal. A voyage that had meant 7,000 miles around the Cape was now only 50 miles across the Isthmus of Panama, from the Atlantic to the Pacific. The Canal divided the land, but it united the world. From the time of Marco Polo and Columbus to Gorgas and Goethals, man's quest for a westward passage to fabled Cathay led to one of the greatest engineering feats in history. The story of the Panama Canal is not only a story of adventure and adventurers, of greed, lust and battle, it is also the story of man's victory over nature, of dedication, loyalty and unbelievable heroism.

The Land Divided, The World United

by PAUL RINK

Drawings by Barry Martin

JULIAN MESSNER, INC.   NEW YORK

Published by Julian Messner, Inc.
8 West 40th Street, New York 18

Published simultaneously in Canada
by The Copp Clark Publishing Co. Limited

© Copyright 1963 by Paul Rink

Fourth Printing, 1964

Printed in the United States of America
Library of Congress Catalog Card No. 63-8644

The Land Divided,
The World United

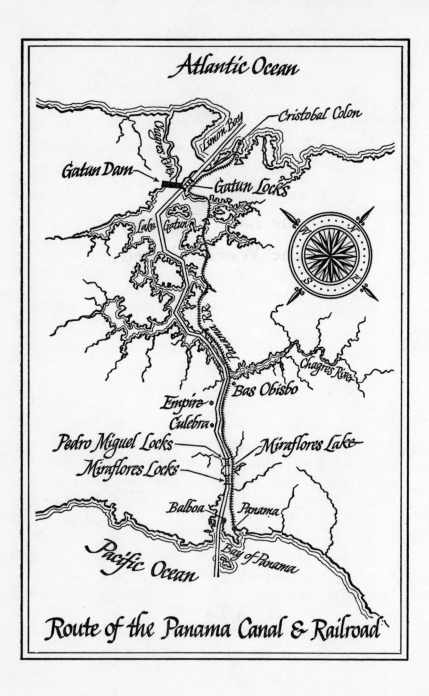

Route of the Panama Canal & Railroad

Chapter 1

Seven A.M., August 15, 1914.

The engine room telegraph of the SS *Ancon* stood at Dead Slow Ahead. The ship trembled gently to the soft thud of machinery and propellers. The only sound was the hiss of water as it slipped past the towering hull.

The big vessel eased out of the channel which leads from Limon Bay on the Atlantic side of the Isthmus of Panama up to the first set of locks at Gatun.

The pilot on the bridge of the *Ancon* gazed aft, took bearings on the channel markers astern. Then he turned and examined the locks which loomed ahead of the ship's bow. The vessel was dwarfed by the formidable gray mass of concrete. In three stupendous steps the locks soared upward and inland. The top level, that of Gatun Lake far above, was a full eighty-five feet higher than the level of the channel where the ship floated.

"Stop the engines."

The quartermaster swung the telegraph handle. Deep below in the engine room, bells clanged. Instantly the trembling of the steel hull ceased. The ship drifted across the water.

The last breath of morning breeze was gone. From the

7

mangrove swamps a reeking miasma of steam rose; palm
fronds drooped listlessly. The sky was a perfect blue, innocent of the towering thunderheads, the flickering heat light-
ning and the growling thunder which would come later.
Today would be a scorcher, but then all days were scorchers
on the Isthmus of Panama.

"Two points to starboard."

The helmsman spun the wheel; the spokes slipped
smoothly past his fingers. Slowly the bow of the *Ancon*
swung in a ponderous arc.

"Steady."

The helmsman checked the swing. The ship drifted on.

The decks of the *Ancon* were jammed with people. Dignitaries in white rubbed shoulders with military men; here
and there the bright splashes of diplomatic uniforms and
decorations gleamed in the sunlight. The massed bands of
the Republic of Panama and the Tenth United States In-
fantry were resplendent; the instruments glittered and
sparkled. The gentle hills and the flat land nearby were
crowded with thousands of people, all equipped with picnic
baskets, hampers and umbrellas against the quick tropic
downpours. Today was a holiday on the Panama Canal Zone.

Now the people were silent, tense, as they watched the
Ancon creeping over the water and easing toward the locks.
Today was the big day. The crucial test. The opening of the
Panama Canal.

This was the day an age-old dream was about to become
a reality. A dream over four hundred years old was at long
last to come true. All these people on the ship and those
crowded ashore knew about this dream. It had been their

dream, the goal toward which they had been laboring for the past ten years.

The question was in everyone's heart: Was this Canal really going to work? Would they succeed where everyone else who had tried to build the Canal had failed? Throughout the long years, each man who was now watching the *Ancon* so intently had performed his task, fought his own struggle. The job had been so huge that individual workers were scarcely aware of what their neighbors had been doing. Today all these separate efforts are united to form one gigantic whole, one smoothly operating finished unit.

Sweat ran down the small of the pilot's back in a steady rivulet. He wiped his palms on the damp linen of his jacket. The drops dripped steadily from the tip of his nose, his elbows. Yes, today was a scorcher, but far more than heat caused the perspiration to spurt in such a torrent.

He peered at the lock approaches. The ship came in very slowly, barely with steerageway. Now was the moment! The pilot gave an order. Heaving lines shot through the air. In seconds anxious hands pulled them back aboard, dragging heavy steel cables which were attached to the mules.

Now the mules—powerful, squat, electric trams running on tracks along the lock walls—took up the slack in the cables and started to move ahead. They were supposed to drag the ship into the locks, stop her once inside, and then keep her centered exactly in the chamber as water flowed in. The ship's power was not to be used—theoretically. Should a vessel crash into a wall or a gate and wreck either herself or the locks while in them, the damage would be beyond calculation.

A full dress rehearsal of this first transit with a big ship had been held two weeks earlier with the SS *Cristobal*, sister ship of the *Ancon*. It had not been a complete success. The mules had great difficulty holding the ship. One had burned out a motor, another had snapped a steel cable. Only by a hair had the vessel been stopped before she crashed into a set of gates. Twenty thousand tons of runaway steel had finally been brought under control—but the memory of the nightmare remained.

Colonel George Washington Goethals, the engineer in charge of all construction and planning, had done much serious soul-searching. He and his marine experts had grimly faced the possibility that the scheme of transit with electric mules—an innovation at which many experienced seafaring men had snorted derisively—simply *might not work*.

Since the first trial, much time had been spent in practice. Certain changes in the procedure were made. Much more power than had been anticipated was needed to bring a large ship to a dead halt, even when she was moving at a scarcely perceptible crawl. More mules had therefore been assigned to each vessel. The permissible approach speeds were cut way down. With all the changes, with much practice and experimentation, and by using extreme caution, it at last seemed possible that handling large vessels in the locks with mules was feasible.

Today, before the eyes of the whole world, a public demonstration of this faith was to be staged.

The *Ancon* crept into the first lock chamber. At precisely the right moment the pilot signaled, and all six mules literally squatted back on their haunches and heaved in unison. The operators' hands were slippery with sweat as they worked the controls of the mules. Easy . . . easy . . . enough strain to do the job but not so much that the cables would snap.

Everything held. The tremendous bulk of the *Ancon* slid to a stop within the distance of a few feet.

There was not a sound from the crowd, only an uneasy release of tension. Although the people ashore could scarcely see the mast tops of the *Ancon* now that she was deep inside the first lock, this glimpse was enough to show that her motion had been halted. The crowd waited, still apprehensive, to see what would happen next.

The gates behind the ship began to swing shut. Gently and smoothly, and in total silence, the giant sections swung together. They met and sealed precisely in the center of the lock. Massive chains rose dripping from the water ahead and astern of the ship and stretched across the lock. Their purpose was to protect the vital gates in case an unexpected surge caused the vessel to move.

Now another signal was given to the control towers and mammoth valves were opened. Water began to flow from the lake far above through great pipes into the lock chamber. As it filled, the ship rose slowly in it.

To the people aboard, it seemed as though they were rising out of a deep pit. To the people ashore, the ship appeared to be emerging from the solid earth itself. As the ship rose the mules carefully reeled in the cables, inch by inch, at all times keeping the necessary tension so that the *Ancon* could not move from her position.

At last the lock was filled. The *Ancon* was on a level with the water in the next, or middle, lock chamber. With the gates astern tightly shut, the forward gates were opened and the mules pulled the ship ahead. More confident now, the operators stopped her neatly. The gates behind swung shut, the chains rose in place, and the whole process was repeated.

And once more! When the forward gates of the top chamber were opened, the ship floated on a level with Gatun Lake, far, far above the Caribbean which lay behind. Ahead stretched the lake—clear sailing to the Pacific, except for the locks at the other end of the Canal through which the operation would be repeated in reverse to lower the vessel.

The crowd took a deep breath. This was it. Surely if the *Ancon* could lock up safely from the sea, she should be able to descend as easily to the Pacific.

The pilot walked to the whistle lanyard and pulled it long and hard. The deep blast from the *Ancon*'s siren roared out over the water, reverberated through the clear tropic air and was lost in the surrounding jungle. Far behind, the scores of ships jammed in Limon Bay, waiting to test their own fortune in these strange new locks, heard the sound and took up the chorus.

The spectators shouted out a mighty welcome of jubilation and triumph. The Panama Canal would work! And they had built it! The bands on the *Ancon* manfully rendered "The Star-Spangled Banner," but the strains were drowned in the cheers and whistles.

A stocky figure in white stood on the lock wall. He rested on his umbrella and grinned.

The pilot leaned far out over the wing of the *Ancon*'s bridge and shouted to Colonel Goethals, "Come on aboard, Colonel. Ride across with us."

Goethals only grinned again and waved the ship on. He would follow her in the "Yellow Peril," his brightly painted little motor scooter which ran on the railroad paralleling the general course of the Canal.

The mules cast off; the telegraph jangled. Under her own power now, the *Ancon* moved swiftly out of the lock into the sparkling waters of Gatun Lake. She headed for the distant mountains, through which she must pass before reaching the Pacific. This continental divide stretches from one end of the Isthmus to the other and is but a low point in the stupendous chain of ranges extending in an unbroken sweep from Alaska to Tierra del Fuego at the tip of South America.

The clear, fresh water flowed smoothly beneath her keel as the miles slipped by. The ship threaded islands, gay with flowers and greenery; she twisted past headlands raucous with the clatter of parrots and monkeys. Along the edges of the shore alligators sunned themselves; the big bulls lumbered off in annoyance at the approach of the vessel. The jungle flowed untouched and primitive out of an immense distance, then halted abruptly and in shock at the water's edge. Occasionally rows of buzzards, hunched like black knobs on the limbs, gazed curiously at the vessel as it swept by, much as their ancestors must have gazed on the creaky little caravels of Columbus as they ventured cautiously along the coast a few miles distant.

A few hours before, the *Ancon* had floated on the ocean. Now she was eighty-five feet above it, gliding on an inland sea. In three gigantic strides through the locks she had climbed this height to a lake that stretched for miles, with vast inlets and bays, a lake that was past believing. When the Canal had been started ten years before, this lake hadn't even existed! The great dam at Gatun which had been built to hold the water in place was now a part of the landscape. Already it was covered with soft grass, and blended beautifully into the surrounding hills. It was a man-made part of the very earth itself, and so naturally did it fit into the scene, no one wondered how it had gotten there.

Along the shores of the lake, at times close by and again in the distance, the thread of the Panama Railroad tracks was visible. Now and then, weaving in and out behind headlands, across bridges, back of hills and through forests, the bright color of the "Yellow Peril" flashed against the green of jungle, as Colonel Goethals shepherded this first big ship through "his" Canal. Completely in keeping with the beloved colonel's personality, he remained on the side lines making sure that everything ran smoothly rather than participating actively in this final triumphant moment.

At last the lake narrowed and the channel entered the cuts through the mountains themselves. As the lake was left behind, on the port side of the ship was the broad mouth of a great river—the Chagres. Never had a river suffered such indignities. It had been rerouted, diverted. It had been subdued, utterly tamed, and its fierce, devastating rampages were only memories. Completely docile now, it poured into the lake to provide the water which moved ships up and down through the locks and to generate electricity. The excess water was permitted to escape harmlessly into the sea.

The *Ancon* glided past the river mouth and entered the continental divide itself. Her speed was reduced; navigation here was apt to be ticklish. Through the cuts the lake was reduced to a narrow nine-mile channel blasted out of almost solid rock—a precise silvery ribbon leading directly and safely to the Pacific. At times the banks of the cut were low; at other places they towered sharp and dangerous far overhead. In these cuts, for decades, starting with the French in 1880, men had labored. Buried in deep gorges, broiled in the heat, drenched in rain, dazzled by the glare of sunlight reflected from brilliant red and lavender walls, they had hacked and scratched and smashed the living stone. How difficult now to believe that all this had taken place! The blasting, the roar of machinery, the endless trains, the thousands of men were all gone. To those aboard the *Ancon* the scene was pastoral. Water and earth and greenery were all that remained to mark the turmoil. The *Ancon*'s wake lapped without harm, like wavelets on some tranquil irrigation ditch, against the sides of the cuts.

At last the pilot slowed the engines. The ship eased up to the locks at Pedro Miguel and was taken in charge by the mules. She entered the lock, the gates closed behind, and the water drained from beneath her. She sank into the earth. The gates opened and she moved majestically out into another lake—tiny Miraflores. The enormous crowds gathered here were silent and apprehensive at first, like those at Gatun. Then they gasped in relief, and shouts of triumph and welcome broke out.

On the Pacific side, the steps of the locks are separated. A single step is located at Pedro Miguel. The other two, built together, are just across the lake from it, at Miraflores.

After a few minutes' sail across the little lake, and a safe passage downward through the locks, the *Ancon* was once more at sea level. With salt water again beneath her keel, she made the run down to the Pacific and headed out past

the breakwater to the islands in Panama Bay—the first official and public transit from ocean to ocean.

The anchorage on the Pacific side, like that on the Caribbean, was crammed with ships from all the maritime nations
of the world. As the *Ancon* passed serenely among them
they greeted her with cheers and with deep throbbing blasts
from their whistles. To these ships—their officers and crews
waiting for their chance to make a transit—the real miracle
of the Canal came alive. To them, if not so much to all of
those who had worked so long to make the dream come true,
it *was* miraculous that the *Ancon,* passing so tranquilly before their eyes, had floated in the Caribbean just a few hours
before. By any way of figuring, by all the charts, by all the
calculations of every navigator who had ever lived, the
Caribbean was 7,000 miles distant! And yet this ship which
glided through the anchored vessels had floated on that sea
some eight hours ago!

The *Ancon* turned and headed back up the channel toward Balboa, the brand-new city of red tile and cement
which the ditchdiggers had built on "spoil," or the diggings
from the Canal cuts. Henceforward, Balboa would be the
capital of the Canal, the administrative headquarters.

Another enormous crowd, headed by jubilant Colonel
Goethals, was on hand at the docks to welcome the ship.
Through the swiftly fading sunlight of the tropic afternoon
she eased slowly into the basin and warped up to the pier.
The voyage was done.

The ten years it took the United States to build the Canal
are only part of the whole story. The complete tale goes
way, way back into the past. Ours was the final effort, the
successful one, but what happened before is also a very real

part. It is a tale of greed, dedication, struggle; of murder, battle, war, cruelty and unbelievable heroism. Some parts of the tale seem to have little to do with digging the "Big Ditch," but they all fit into the saga of men who traveled as they inched their way toward this bright August 15, 1914.

As the lines were made fast to the dock and the *Ancon* finally came to rest, as the speeches were made and the bands played and people cheered and sang themselves hoarse with the joy of victory, twilight fell. The blue mists seemed alive with ghosts—the ghosts of all those before who had dreamed and planned and walked through the luminous evenings of Panama.

Chapter 2

It was early in the year 1502, and the four tiny caravels seemed lost on the immensity of the sea. Their sails were insignificant particles beneath the enormous arc of sky, the rolling clouds and the soaring mountains of the land which lay ahead. Driven by the steady dry-season winds, the vessels danced smoothly over the Caribbean swells toward the smudge of coast which lay in the distance.

On the flagship a sailor ran rapidly aft, his bare feet sure and quick on the heaving deck. He tumbled down a short ladder and knocked at the door of a cabin.

"Admiral," he panted, with urgency in his voice. "Admiral!"

The door opened. A tall, emaciated man, old and obviously ill, but with the gleam of a visionary in his eyes, stood in the doorway.

"Admiral," said the sailor, "A very large canoe . . . just ahead. With many Indians. Unlike any we have seen before."

The old man hurried up to the deck, eyes blinking in the blazing sunshine. Nearby floated the strange canoe. It was indeed very large. Long lines of paddlers manned each side, and in the stern under a palm thatch, lolled the captain, gently fanning himself. The Indians were all neatly dressed

18

in white or in brightly colored cotton blouses, and the ornaments in their noses, ears, around their necks and arms gleamed dully but unmistakably golden. They gazed with astonishment at the Spanish ships.

An order was given. Sails were backed. The caravels drifted.

"It seems to be a merchant, Admiral," said one of the Spanish officers, noting that the midship section of the canoe was piled high with trade goods—baskets, cloth, knives, hatchets, ornaments, pottery, cacao beans.

The admiral nodded. "We come in peace," he said, and turned to his men. "Put down your weapons. We will trade."

A few beads and trinkets were exchanged for the golden ornaments, which the Spaniards examined carefully. Their eyes glittered as they noted the thickness and weight of the metal rather than the delicate designs and superb workmanship.

"Where has it come from?" they asked.

The trader-captain of the canoe gestured vaguely to the south. There was something about these people with their light eyes and skin, and their big ships, that he didn't like. Directly ashore was his home—the ancient and rich kingdom of the Mayans in Yucatan. By sending the strangers to the south he probably saved his land from immediate conquest.

One more question was laboriously put to him by sign language and interpreters: "Is there a channel for ships across this land?"

The Indian pondered; again he pointed to the south. "There is," he said, "a narrow place between two seas."

Sails were hoisted on the caravels. With the land on the starboard side, they picked up speed and headed southward, each man in the four tossing cockleshells intent on a dream. Most shared the same dream. In each head swam a vision of gold—thick and heavy, like that of the ornaments.

The tall old man sat in his cabin. He too had a dream, a very ancient dream. His vision was of "a narrow place between two seas." As night fell and lamps were lit, his face glowed with the strength of his dream. "A narrow place between two seas," chanted his heart, and in the distance lay Cathay—*his* particular dream.

The roots of the dream that brought Christopher Columbus in 1502 to the Caribbean coast of Central America lay deep in the past.

For centuries before the birth of Christ, and for a thousand years after, highly advanced cultures rose and fell in the lands of the East. Throughout all these years, the people of Europe were slowly lifting themselves out of barbarism. Eventually life in each of these two worlds—the West and the East—met. Men traded with each other.

Great seaport cities grew in the eastern Mediterranean. Long, plodding camel caravans came out of the old "Silk Roads" across the deserts. The merchandise they carried was reshipped to the rising civilizations of Europe. Such cities as Venice, Alexandria and Aleppo flourished on this commerce.

With eager, greedy eyes the people who lived in the dark castles, in the cold and dirty medieval European cities, gazed upon the wonders which had come to them from such a vast distance! Eagerly they desired to possess them.

Never had their senses feasted on such magnificence. There were jewels worth the ransom of a queen—diamonds, opals, blazing emeralds, pale cat-eyes; magnificent weapons

—swords and lances made of unbelievably tough steel, light but strong armor; strange and exciting fabrics—snowy linens, heavy satins, silks shimmering and fragile as moonlight. And to give their rough diet of meat and bread new exciting flavors there were spices—cloves, cinnamon, nutmeg, cardamom, pepper and many others. In addition to all this, there came knowledge! Word of ancient religions, philosophies and manuscripts on mathematics, physiology, astronomy and chemistry whetted the minds of scholars.

The word of eyewitnesses began coming back. In the eleventh, twelfth and thirteenth centuries returning Crusaders brought stories of the wonders they had seen with their own eyes. In the late twelfth century, Marco Polo, son of a great Venetian trading family, went deep into the Orient. He ventured farther than any Westerner had ever gone before—clear to the land of the Kublai Khan. He came home with incredible tales of the knowledge and opulence beyond the deserts and mountains.

The trade between the East and the West grew and prospered, but at the same time something else was happening. The Europeans were well out of their rough beginnings. They began to think for themselves and to invent their own ideas about the world. Naturally they came to hope that there might be another way, a water route perhaps, to the Orient.

A great Portuguese thinker, Prince Henry, started a school of navigation in Lisbon. To it he attracted mapmakers and geographers, the best navigators, the finest mathematicians and philosophers he could find. Slowly the store of knowledge in this school grew. New concepts about the size and the shape of the earth were advanced. Painful but sure

progress was made in the science of navigation by the stars. Yearly, flimsy little Portuguese ships ventured farther and farther from home. They generally sailed to the south, along the unknown and forbidding coast of Africa.

Prince Henry died in 1460 but seven years before his death, in 1453, an event took place which was like the dropping of the curtain on an act of an absorbing drama. The Turks conquered Constantinople and immediately blocked off the old desert trade routes. The two worlds were separated, isolated from each other.

Finding a new route to the Orient now became a necessity for the Europeans. It was no longer just a fascinating exercise in geography for an intelligent and curious Portuguese prince.

Since the time of the ancient Greeks, certain "crackpots" had insisted that the world might, of all things, be round! If this were really so, then most certainly the Indies could be reached by sailing far enough in a westerly direction.

Down the centuries thinkers and philosophers persisted in their belief of this radical theory. The notion was pretty farfetched, and nobody took its advocates very seriously. In order to prove it, an actual voyage would have to be made, and what sovereign in his right mind would give permission for such a foolhardy trip, much less put up the money to finance it?

In 1478 a man appeared who refused to take no for an answer. His ideas about the shape of the earth were so firmly fixed in his mind that he dedicated his entire life to them. He was an experienced young Genoese sailor named Christopher Columbus.

He begged, pleaded, argued for fourteen long years.

Finally, in 1492, he convinced the court of Spain that he might be worth backing. Legend says that Queen Isabella had to pawn her royal jewels to raise the money.

The little flotilla which sailed from Spain consisted of three small caravels—the *Niña*, the *Pinta* and the *Santa Maria*. There were eighty-three timid, quaking souls aboard, many of them convicts who had been given pardons in return for signing up. Even so, it had been difficult to man the ships. Not many were willing to exchange prison for the terrors of such a voyage.

They discovered the West Indies and returned home to royal honors. On the second voyage a large colony of 1,500 men was established on the island of Santo Domingo. It was the first European settlement in the Western Hemisphere.

Still obsessed by the dream of a western passage, Columbus explored the coast of South America on his third voyage. These new lands which white men were seeing for the first time were beautiful . . . and enchanted. Columbus recorded Venezuela as near the Garden of Eden. The torrent of fresh water flowing seaward from the mighty Orinoco River he felt sure was the overflow from the fountain which waters the Tree of Life! Another river he identified as the Ganges. A large peninsula was thought to be the kingdom of Siam.

Columbus' discoveries had produced little—tales of endless leagues of a vast, empty land which seemed to stretch father than any man could hope to sail, and a few golden trinkets, a few pearls, some exotic feather costumes and a handful of outlandish Indians. A small reward indeed for the expense. The aging explorer never lost his faith, but in spite of all he could do, interest in the New World languished.

Then an event took place which once more brought him and his dreams into the limelight. In 1498, Vasco da Gama, a mariner trained in the great school of Prince Henry, rounded the tip of Africa. He called it the Cape of Good Hope, after the old dream that perhaps it might just be the "cape of the good hope of the Indies." Soon his little vessel lay swinging on her anchor in the swarming harbor of Calcutta. She was the first European ship to reach the Indies.

The old Mediterranean ports, already hard hit by the blockage of the desert routes, were now doomed. With the very reason for their life gone they sank into an oblivion which lasted for three centuries. Proud new western cities, like Lisbon, prospered. Even Venice was obliged to buy her pepper in the Lisbon markets. The wealth of the Orient arrived in Europe by water.

The Mediterranean was now a blind alley, leading nowhere. The future belonged to the Atlantic seafaring powers —Portugal, France, Spain, Holland and England. The rivalry among them was intense. Their eyes turned westward. Once again Spain outfitted a fleet for the aging Columbus and he sailed on his fourth and last voyage. This was in 1502.

As the little squadron set its sails for the south and left the coast of Yucatan behind, Columbus' hopes were high. What else could "a narrow place between the seas" mean but the passage to Cathay? The ships passed what is now the coast of Nicaragua, Honduras and Costa Rica, exploring as they went. At last they came to the Isthmus of Panama. As they poked and probed through the islands and inlets of the vast Chiriqui Lagoon and Almirante Bay, hopes were always high that just around the next peninsula or back of the next sand bar, the waters would open westward. Wishing could not make it true. Always ahead of the bows of the ships, mountains rose endlessly into the west.

Columbus attempted to establish a fort, the first white settlement on the mainland, and left his brother in command. No sooner were the ships out of sight than the Indians massacred the little garrison to the last man.

A terrible hurricane drove one of the vessels ashore with great loss of life. In the three remaining ships, the voyage was continued.

By now the rainy season had come, with its storms and crashing torrents of water that poured ceaselessly from a leaden sky. The expedition passed the winter ashore in Veraguas, a pleasant land of open savannas with abundant food. The Indians were gentle, and possessed some gold. Columbus and his men passed the time agreeably, resting and filling their purses.

When the dry season came once more, they headed southward again. Exploring Limon Bay, the noses of the ships poked tentatively into the Chagres River, but it didn't look too likely. Had Columbus sailed up the river he would have been the first white man to explore the route over which the Panama Canal was eventually built.

Still further along they found a beautiful, land-locked harbor, with deep, calm water. They called it Puerto Bello, or beautiful port. Here in Portobelo, as it came to be called, a second ship was left rotting on the beach, its timbers honeycombed by *teredo* worms.

With the rainy season once more upon them. Columbus

was forced to give up the search. In the two overcrowded ships, with scant food, he set sail for Santo Domingo. Heavy-hearted, he watched the coast recede behind him. The Isth-mus—the "narrow place between the seas"—had indeed been discovered, but it was not what he had thought it would be.

The search for the elusive strait was continued by the sailors of many nations. The Cabots, Amerigo Vespucci, Magellan, Henry Hudson, led an interminable parade of ships and mariners scouring the coasts of the Americas from Labrador to Cape Horn, looking for the strait. Dutch, French, Portuguese, English and, of course, Spanish planted their flags wherever they could find a toehold. Eventually men realized that these lands were not a part of Asia, nor were they a chain of islands. They were great continents. Hope for the Westward Passage died hard though, and in 1507, the first map ever printed of the New World showed an open strait about where the Isthmus of Panama is located.

Before long a new discovery made in the Spanish settle-ments on the Isthmus took precedence over everything else. Gold! Eternal rivers of gold! Why search for mythical pas-sages or worry about Cathay?

Tough, resourceful fighting men were needed to conquer the Indians and bring back their wealth in gold. Spain had them in abundance. The country had just finished a long struggle for freedom from the Moors and was filled with experienced, hard-bitten veterans.

There was little trouble filling the ranks of the legions which sailed westward. In one stroke impoverished noble-men and gold-hungry adventurers could bring lands and glory and gold to their mother-country, and fill their own pockets at the same time! Stout Spanish hearts and swords clamored to sail west!

In 1500, thousands of Indians lived on the Isthmus. They were of many different tribes and spoke different languages. The one thing they had in common doomed them all: they mined and used a great deal of gold and silver.

Suddenly, to their bewilderment they were set upon by murderous invaders, clad in armor, riding great animals, leading fierce and hungry dog packs. In their hands the invaders carried a quick death that was accompanied by a thunderous noise. They discovered that these strangers attached value only to one thing—gold. To get it they killed, murdered, tortured and made slaves of the entire Indian population. The tribes were incensed by the lust and cruelty and rose up and fought the Spanish with all their strength.

The fighting during these murderous years, however, was not only between the Spanish and the native population. Soon the Spanish were fighting each other. Among them were many cruel, lustful and arrogant men who would tolerate no interference. They had come for gold, and didn't care how they got it.

As the years passed, the abuse of the Indians and the looting of the land increased in fury. The river of gold which sailed for Spain in the clumsy galleons increased to a flood. The hordes of treasure-hungry adventurers grew. A few of them returned to Spain to live like kings. Many died miserably, victims of fever, wounds, poisonous reptiles.

As Spain began to realize the fantastic riches of these lands she had blundered upon, a Council of the Indies was set up for their administration. The ideals were lofty, but communications were slow and uncertain. Besides, who would ever punish a swaggering *conquistador* for sending home too much gold? Forget about how he had gotten it!

Many of the Spanish governors were able and decent men, but they were helpless to control the avaricious and cruel. Often these good men came to an untimely end. Such a one was Vasco Nuñez de Balboa.

An impoverished but gay and handsome young *hidalgo*, he stowed away on an expedition in a cask marked "victuals for the voyage." So capable was this stowaway that he rose to be head of the expedition, and eventually governor of the colonies. He was practical and tough, a good soldier, but also intelligent and humane. He understood that more gold could be obtained by cooperation with the Indians than by excessive stark brutality.

Balboa was the first man to look upon the Pacific Ocean. He determined to sail across it to a land in which, according to the Indians, people ate and drank from dishes of solid gold. He constructed a fleet of four small brigantines, dismantled them, and with the assistance of thousands of Indian slaves carried them across the Isthmus and launched them on the Pacific. All unknowingly, he prepared to sail for Peru, when a messenger arrived from the governor, known as Pedrarias the Cruel.

Balboa returned to the capital for a conference with Pedrarias, who promptly imprisoned him in a cage, paraded him through the streets of the town and later beheaded him.

Meantime, some reliable means of communication across the Isthmus had to be developed. The capital of the colony was moved to a site near the present city of Panama. *Panama La Vieja*, or Old Panama, it was called, and speedily it became the "Cup of Gold," the brightest jewel in the crown of Spain. A road was built by slaves across the Isthmus, from the city to the squalid little port of Nombre de Dios, which means "in the name of God," on the Atlantic side. Over this trail stumbled the long pack trains, laboring, sweating, goaded by the soldiers. Indians and a few mules carried the treasure. The road was called Las Cruces Trail—the Trail of the Crossing—and it is still there today.

Panama City increased in importance. In addition to the officials and the soldiers, many merchants and their families flocked to the city from Europe. They dealt in slaves, cloth, gold, silver and spices. Much trade was built up between Spain and the Orient, and it all flowed through Panama.

Eventually men found out for certain that there was no water route connecting the two oceans. By 1520 agitation to build such a route had started. The great Hernando Cortez, when he saw the Isthmus, said, "As long as God has not seen fit to join these two oceans, then let man do the job himself." Such a task seemed child's play to the man who had conquered Montezuma, the great Aztec chief, and delivered the Aztec kingdom to Spain.

In 1517, Alonzo de Saavedra, an early engineer, began to make surveys. Under the prodding of Charles V, they continued. Saavedra urged an eight-foot channel, but he did so with no idea of the difficulties which even such a modest canal would involve.

Francisco Pizarro, an illiterate swineherd who rose to power, conquered Peru in 1524, and the stream of gold flow-

ing from there to the Isthmus and hence to Spain turned
into a torrent. Now it became urgent that an easier way
across the Isthmus than Las Cruces Trail had to be found.

In 1534, Pascual de Andagoya, governor of Panama, made
another survey. He reported that the project was feasible
and that it should follow the route of the Chagres River
from the Atlantic to its headwaters and then should be dug
the rest of the way to the Pacific. Andagoya wisely added
that to do so would probably exhaust the richest treasury in
all of Christendom!

Several other routes—in Panama, in Nicaragua and in
Mexico—were also explored. All the plans came to nothing.
In spite of the need, and regardless of how much money or
lives might be spent, the task was simply beyond the abil-
ities of the times.

So the old land routes across Mexico and Las Cruces Trail
across Panama were strengthened, fortified and kept in re-
pair. By 1556, King Charles' son Philip was on the throne
of Spain, and he shrewdly reversed the policy of his government. He realized he had better let well enough alone.
The construction of a canal probably would not really increase the river of gold from Peru. Las Cruces Trail might
be difficult, but it worked well enough. Furthermore, such
a canal would be most vulnerable to Spain's growing host of
envious and powerful enemies. No doubt it would be the
better part of wisdom to keep a solid wall of earth between
the source of the gold and enemy ships. Philip forbade any
further mention of a canal under penalty of death! There
was to be no more talk or surveys on the subject. The Church
loyally upheld the decision of the king.

At the same time, this rich New World was under determined attack from many different quarters. Spain had her hands full just hanging on to what she had, let alone expending blood and treasure on the building of a canal. A canal would have been of little benefit to Spain but would surely have aided her enemies. King Philip had been very wise. For two hundred years this subject was taboo in Spain.

Chapter 3

When Spain conquered these lands of the New World who could possibly have forseen that within a very few years, all of Latin America, from Mexico to Peru, would turn into a gigantic fountain of gold and silver? It spilled out a flood of treasure that was the envy of the entire world.

Systematically Spain looted her empire, but this empire which had been hard won was harder to keep intact. There was never a moment's peace.

The Indian populations had been defeated and enslaved, but time after time the anguished peoples rose up against their masters, killing and murdering. Bands of slaves, called *cimarrones,* which means wild or untamed, often escaped to the forests and established small settlements with but one idea in mind: to kill Spaniards. One of the *cimarron* chieftains named Bayano successfully resisted the Spanish for years. Determined to get rid of this pest, the governor sent a large expedition against him. It was so soundly trounced that only four Spaniards lived to stagger back to civilization and tell their harrowing story. Today there is a river in eastern Panama called the Bayano, in memory of this early freedom fighter.

As Spain raked in the treasure and fought off Indians with

one hand, the other was very soon busy fighting off furious attacks which came from a different quarter.

Sea raiders were attracted to the Isthmus like hornets to a feast. For a hundred and fifty years they buzzed angrily along the coasts and through the islands of the Caribbean.

These raiders were of every color and nationality. Some were "respectable." They operated as privateers and flew England's red Union Jack or the tricolor of France. Others hid their identity. Still others made no attempt to conceal their profession. From the mastheads of their swift ships flapped the skull and crossbones.

The pirates—called buccaneers because their principal item of diet was salted goat meat which they dried on frames called *boucones*—were highly organized, with their own supply routes and depots. They even had a system of accident insurance which recompensed their members for wounds received in battle. For certain very hazardous ventures, the rates were increased—"double indemnity." Fifteen hundred pieces of eight were paid for the loss of both legs. Both hands were worth 1,800 pieces. The loss of a single leg or hand brought only 600 pieces, while one eye was rated at only 100! Perhaps the traditional pirate's wooden leg, metal hook in place of a hand, or eye patch were not regarded as any particular inconvenience.

Spanish reaction to these predators was swift and violent. Any non-Spanish ship, regardless of flag, was sunk and her crew sold into slavery. Fleets of warships patrolled the coasts and waters approaching Panama. The ransom of a kingdom was poured into armies and fortresses spread from one end to the other of her huge, scattered empire.

All this was little deterrent. When a prize is great enough, desperate men are always available to take the risks. What greater prize could be imagined than a deep-laden Spanish galleon wallowing home to Castile? As fast as a raider was caught, two more seemed to pop up.

Frantically, the Spanish carted their treasure over the Andes and shipped it from Cartagena. Raiders simply waited beyond the bulge of the continent off what is now the coast of Venezuela. Masters of other Spanish ships tried the long route around South America, but the pirates lurked among the islands of Tierra del Fuego and many a battle was fought to a finish on the black, icy seas off Cape Horn.

The plate ships, those carrying the treasure, were ordered to travel in groups. No matter—the raiders attacked in groups. The Spanish Admiralty built powerful warships to convoy the "platers" across the Atlantic, and for a few years all went well. However, the peace was short-lived. There was no stopping the invaders. The loot was golden, rich beyond the wildest dreams, and the territory was too vast for effective defense.

Vultures from half of Europe roved the Spanish Main. They began going after the settlements themselves—on the mainland and on the islands. The time came when colonists trembled and ran for their guns at the sight of any strange sail on the horizon. Ultimately the Spanish were actually outnumbered. What they had won by drenching the land with Indian blood they now had to try to defend with rivers of their own.

French corsairs, led by the ferocious and bloodthirsty L'Olonais, looted the great fortresses of Santiago and Havana on the island of Cuba. L'Olonais later met his death on the mainland at the hands of Darien Indians, implacable foes of all white men. English sea-robbers and Dutch *zee roovers*, singly and at times in joint effort, looted gold-mining towns in Veraguas.

This blood bath of pillage, looting, murder and carnage on the high seas started very soon after the Spanish made their initial discoveries. Scattered raids had taken place from the very beginning, but the curtain really went up about the middle of the sixteenth century—that is, a scant fifty or sixty years after Columbus. What happened paved the way for all that was to come and eventually resulted in open warfare between Spain and England.

In 1560, a small flotilla of English merchant ships delivered a cargo of slaves from Africa to various ports in the Caribbean. At this early date, the native populations had already been so thinned out that the Spanish had to import Negro slaves to work the mines and plantations. The commander of this fleet of slavers was Admiral Sir John Hawkins. The captain of one of his smaller ships—the *Judith*, of about fifty tons—was his young nephew, Francis Drake. Drake was the son of a Devonshire preacher, and he had early felt the call of the sea. After serving an apprenticeship before the mast, he rose to command, and at this time had already accompanied his uncle on a number of slaving voyages.

Badly battered by a hurricane, and desperately short of water, the little fleet of four vessels was driven clear back to San Juan de Ulua, the port for Veracruz, in Mexico. The captain of the port assured Hawkins that he would not be molested while the ships were watered and repaired. However, just when Hawkins was preparing to set sail for home, a powerful squadron of Spanish war vessels arrived in the port to convoy the plate ships to Spain. The Spanish admiral promptly opened fire and practically blew the English ships out of the water. Only the *Judith* and one other small brig escaped. From this point on Francis Drake nursed a permanent grudge against everything Spanish.

By 1572 he had gathered a group of tough, hard-bitten fighting men about him and sailed for the Spanish colonies. He went, not as a pirate, but as a privateer, flying the English flag.

His first objective was the fortified gold port of Nombre de Dios. After fierce, bloody fighting he and his men reached the center of town but were finally repulsed at the very doors of the king's treasure house. The sight of gold and silver bars stacked like cordwood in the streets and gold dust shoveled into bins like grain was too much for his men. After convalescing, they again attacked and were again beaten off.

The rainy season had set in and rather than go after Nombre de Dios directly, Drake decided to capture a mule train on Las Cruces Trail. He was joined by over seventy French corsairs and a huge mob of wild *cimarrones*. Slipping, stumbling, sweating, beating their way through the dripping jungle they succeeded, after a first disastrous attempt, in capturing a rich train.

Drake got away with his loot and proudly sailed into Plymouth Harbor in England on a bright Sunday morning. Rich, successful, and promoted to admiral, he made a voyage around the world in the *Golden Hind*, not forgetting to burn and loot Spanish fortresses wherever he could find them. When he returned again to England, Queen Elizabeth knighted him on the deck of his ship.

Stung to fury, the Spanish used a part of their own loot to

build a great armada in 1588 and launch it against England. Drake had a hand in defeating the squadron as it sailed up the English Channel.

Back again in the Western Hemisphere, planning on capturing the entire Isthmus of Panama, he sacked Nombre de Dios and started across Las Cruces Trail for Panama City. The Spanish were not asleep, however, and they so harried and ambushed the English that Drake and his men were lucky to escape back to their ships.

On the way to Nicaragua to recuperate, and to see what they could pick up in the treasure houses there, Drake fell ill with dysentery and died. His uniform and his weapons were sealed with his body in a leaden casket, and his sorrowing crew buried him at sea off Portobelo.

The Spaniards abandoned Nombre de Dios and moved the town bodily to the heavily fortified port of Portobelo. More castles with great walls were built and huge cannon were set in place, but the glittering prize was too tempting for desperate men. All the cannon in the world couldn't keep them away.

One of the most notorious predators of all was Captain Henry Morgan. Unlike Drake, who was a privateer and flew the English flag, Morgan was an out-and-out buccaneer and conducted his raids beneath the skull and crossbones flag of the pirate brotherhoods.

Morgan was a Welshman by birth. He was a small man, soft-spoken and mild in appearance, but the murderous ferocity of his raids kept the Spanish in a turmoil for years. Extremely audacious, he seemed to regard the entire Caribbean as his own private hunting ground. He ranged from one end to the other and the harassed defenders never knew where or when to expect him.

As a young boy, Henry had been kidnapped, sold into slavery and sent to the Spanish plantations on Jamaica. During these years he learned to hate his masters and also acquired much valuable information about them and their possessions. He finally escaped and found safety with the pirates in their strongholds. Burning with hatred for the Spanish, a skillful seaman and courageous, he rose rapidly to command ships and men of his own. By 1665 he was ready for really big undertakings.

He had long had his eye on the fortress of San Lorenzo, located on a bluff overlooking the mouth of the Chagres River in Limon Bay. San Lorenzo was a gold port; here treasure was accumulated for transshipment to Spain. It was a rich enough plum to tempt any gang of cutthroats, but only a chieftain as well armed and as daring as Morgan could think of attacking it. San Lorenzo was very powerful. Its stone battlements were towering and massive; a deep moat protected the landward side. The defenders were well armed with cannon, muskets and ammunition.

Morgan waited until patrolling Spanish warships were out of the vicinity and then he attacked. On a hot afternoon during the dry season, a flotilla of pirate longboats discharged men and equipment on a little beach near the mouth of the river. Coolly Morgan directed his men and ordered their charge up the hill.

Just as coolly the Spanish commander directed the defense. His position, so he thought, was impregnable. He waited until the pirates were halfway up, and then he opened fire with a murderous storm of cannon shot, rifle fire and arrows.

The screaming pirates were pinned down. The air was filled with dust, greasy black smoke, shouts, oaths. Morgan urged his men on. Inch by inch, and with very heavy casualties, they wormed their way up the hill, dragging small assault cannon behind them.

Finally, by nightfall, the pirates were stopped. They could advance no farther. The gleeful Spanish hurled insults and taunts at the "English dogs," inviting them to attack. The battle seemed over.

A tremendous stroke of luck favored Morgan. A Spanish crossbowman took careful aim at a bearded pirate ruffian, and pulled the trigger. The man was hit and knocked down, but before he died, he got to his feet and pulled the bolt from his chest. He wrapped a bit of cotton around it, rammed it home in his musket and fired at the castle. The cotton caught fire and ignited the thatch roof of a small hut back of the walls. The flames spread and against the flickering light the pirates could spot the Spanish working their guns and picked them off by the dozen.

Even now, the defenders beat off attack after attack. As Morgan and his lieutenants tried to decide what to do, luck again solved their problem. The fire reached San Lorenzo's powder magazine, which exploded, blowing men, buildings and guns sky-high. In a few moments the battle was over.

Out of the garrison of 400 men, only 37 were left alive. Of these, a tiny handful escaped into the jungle to make their way across the Isthmus to Panama City to report the defeat. The rest threw themselves off the bluff into the sea rather than surrender to the doubtful mercies of the pirates.

The victors settled down to lick their wounds, to drink

and to feast their eyes on the glittering contents of the royal treasure house.

By now Henry Morgan had risen in the pirate ranks until he commanded a whole fleet of ships. He whetted his appetite for loot with the sacking of San Lorenzo. Then, in 1668, just before the arrival of the warships from Spain which were coming to escort the platers home, he attacked Portobelo itself. Driving old men, children, women and nuns before his yelling hordes, he finally succeeded in taking the town, killing the defenders nearly to the last man. The warehouses were overflowing. While 175 mules staggered under the weight of the gold, carrying the loot to his ships, he busied himself fighting off a Spanish army that had come from Panama City. Morgan and his men finally escaped and sailed off to the island of Jamaica, a former Spanish colony that had been captured by the English. Before leaving, he sent word to the astonished and infuriated Spanish governor in Panama that he would soon visit *him*.

Morgan kept his word. Three years later he landed at the mouth of the Chagres and again overran the fortress of San Lorenzo. He had thirty-seven ships and over two thousand men.

Leaving a garrison at San Lorenzo, he took twelve hundred men and started for Panama City. After a gory battle, the "Cup of Gold" lay at his mercy. The pirates drank, looted, burned and tortured for twenty-eight days, then left the city a smoldering ruin and returned to San Lorenzo.

Morgan convinced his exhausted men that they deserved a little celebration. He broke out the casks of rum and soon most of them were dead drunk. Morgan then loaded the best of the treasure on his own ship and sailed away to England!

At this time Spain and England had a treaty which guaranteed against such raids and so the British government dutifully clapped Morgan prisoner in the Tower of London. But . . . who could be punished for bringing home too much gold? Shortly Morgan was released and knighted! As Sir Henry Morgan, the wily old buccaneer returned to Jamaica as governor, presumably charged with the task of preventing any more such raids as his. Morgan had indeed done very well by himself.

Panama City was never rebuilt. Like Nombre de Dios, it was moved bodily several miles further down the coast, to the site of the present city. Heavily fortified, it was never captured, although many pirates made the attempt. The new city never attained the opulence and the splendor of the old "Cup of Gold."

The bottom of Spain's treasure chest was still a long way down, but after Morgan's raid, the number of plate ships sailing for home diminished. Even the wealth and the gold of Spanish America was not inexhaustible.

As the treasure dwindled, the audacity of Spain's enemies increased. In 1698 a Scotsman named William Patterson— the man who had founded the Bank of England—conceived the idea of establishing a great colony on the Isthmus. Landings were made and a town built near the old city of Acla where Balboa had been beheaded. Before a combination of climate, Spanish soldiers and hate-filled Indians defeated the dream, over two thousand lives and four million dollars had been thrown away. Nothing remains of the scheme today except names on a map—Caledonia Bay and a suburb of the modern city of Panama called Caledonia.

In 1739 British Admiral Vernon captured Portobelo but

two years later was repulsed in an attack on Cartagena. From now on the dwindling fleets of plate ships all sailed around the Horn.

Mines were exhausted on the Isthmus. The old Las Cruces Trail sank into disrepair and the cities—Panama, Portobelo and the others which had been so rich and so seething with life—sank into a dreaming sleep which was to last a hundred and fifty years.

Spain made a last effort to regain her glory. The edict that any talk about a canal was punishable by death was repealed. In the mid-1700's she sent a royal commission to Nicaragua to make a detailed survey for a waterway. The report was unfavorable, but along with this commission had been two English secret agents. They reported to their government that the project was feasible, and would not be very difficult.

England sent a fleet to Nicaragua under the command of a young captain who was later to achieve eternal fame elsewhere—Horatio Nelson. Nelson's report read:

In order to give facility to the great object of government I intend to possess the Lake of Nicaragua, which, for the present, may be looked upon as the inland Gibraltar of Spanish America. As it commands the only water pass between the oceans, its situation must ever render it a principal post to insure passage to the Southern Ocean, and, by our possession of it, Spanish America is divided in two.

Nelson defeated the dispirited Spanish garrisons but was himself in turn defeated by the climate. All but ten of the crew of his flagship, the *Hinchbrook,* were buried of fever.

Acutely conscious of her dwindling world power, Spain continued to promote a canal project. She sent out survey after survey, and considered three routes: across Mexico at Tehuantepec, in Nicaragua, and in Darien on the Isthmus of Panama. They all came to nothing.

Alexander von Humboldt, a famous German scientist and explorer, also made surveys for a canal. He outlined nine possible routes. The one which he considered to be the most likely followed the old treasure road from Panama City into the mountains, and then down the Chagres to the sea. A century later the whole world would know how accurately he had worked.

Trusting Humboldt's survey more than any of their own, Spain actually directed that a canal be built at this point in 1814. Alas, she had delayed too long. The centuries of greed and cruelty and indifference reaped their harvest. The long-oppressed colonies burned with the desire for freedom and flamed into open rebellion. "Creole" patriots, as those Spanish were called who had been born in the colonies, led armies of insurrection against the mother country.

Two revolutionary movements started simultaneously. In the south, the rebels were led by General San Martin, from Argentina, and in the north, by Simon Bolivar, a Venezuelan. These two forces never joined; each achieved its objectives independently of the other. By 1822, after ten years of some of the bitterest and bloodiest fighting the world has ever seen, Central and South America were free. Spain had lost her chance.

The lively little nations of Central America—Guatemala, Honduras, Salvador, Nicaragua and Costa Rica—formed a union, but it seemed they could agree on only one thing: they wanted a canal built and the only possible builder was the swiftly growing nation to the north, the United States of America.

They sent representatives to Washington, suggesting a treaty. Secretary of State Henry Clay expressed "deep interest," but the project died.

From now on, proposals and counterproposals for the construction of a canal flew thick and fast, and they involved some of the most unlikely people imaginable. In most of them the growing interest of the United States was discernible.

The Central American states interested a French promoter named Beninski. Beninski transferred his concession to a New Yorker named De Witt Clinton. Clinton seemed logical as he had successfully managed the Erie Canal, built in the United States in 1825, connecting the Hudson River with Lake Erie. The project collapsed.

Next, Holland entered into an agreement with the government of Nicaragua but abandoned the plan when the United States objected on the grounds that the Monroe Doctrine was violated. This famous "doctrine" has guided our government in its relations with foreign countries for many, many years. President James Monroe spelled it out in his annual message to Congress on December 2, 1823. Very briefly it states that the American continents should no longer be considered as subjects for any new European colonization and that any such attempts would be regarded as unfriendly acts toward the United States. The Doctrine posted a clear "keep out" sign along the coasts of the Western Hemisphere, particularly those of Latin America.

Simon Bolivar in succession granted concessions to a Frenchman, an Englishman and finally to a Swedish engineer. Everybody wanted a canal, but nobody knew exactly what to do about it!

In 1833 the United States took a really serious look southward. President Andrew Jackson sent Charles Biddle to make surveys for a canal. Biddle didn't know much about canals, but he did understand railroads. He went directly to Panama where he entered into private talks for the construction of a rail route across the Isthmus. This, also, came to nothing.

In 1844 Nicaragua broached the subject to King Louis Philippe of France. He wasn't interested, but Louis Napoleon Bonaparte, later Napoleon III, pricked up his ears. He was in jail at the time but he promised that if he were given his freedom, he would from then on interest himself in canal building instead of French politics! One more project collapsed.

Meantime, the United States was rapidly growing westward, and far-seeing people began to clamor, although quietly, for our government to do something. By 1846 we had a treaty with New Granada, of which Panama was a province, for exclusive rights of transit across the Isthmus from Costa Rica to the Gulf of Darien. In return, we promised to defend the country against foreign aggression.

Great Britain claimed all the land along the Caribbean coast of Nicaragua, which included the possible starting points for a canal in *that* area. When she began to show interest in Fonseca Bay, the logical Pacific terminus for a waterway, the United States objected. The two countries came close to war and it was only averted by the famous Clayton-Bulwer treaty of 1850, under the terms of which England gave up her plans.

Meanwhile, an event occurred which altered everything.

Ironically, it was the same thing which had driven the Spaniards through the jungles and old trails. Gold! Gold had been discovered in California. Men, by the thousands, were on their way to make a fortune in the gravelly streams of the West.

Once more transportation across the Isthmus of Panama became vital, and gold was the spur which finally produced action.

Chapter 4

There were three routes to California from our East Coast. A man could go across the continent, presumably on his own two feet if he had to. He could take a ship for the long, uncomfortable and dangerous voyage around Cape Horn, or he could make the "pleasant voyage to Panama, stroll across the fifty miles of Isthmus to the Pacific and, after another easy sea voyage, find himself in San Francisco."

So read the advertisements of the day. The trip wasn't quite like this, but no matter. The pot of gold was just over the horizon.

In no time at all, a human avalanche hit the Isthmus. Panama literally exploded out of its somnolence. Nobody knows how many tens of thousands of men crossed, or tried to cross, during the years of the gold rush. A count made during just *one* dry season showed three to four thousand people attempting the journey each week.

The coast along the Caribbean in the late 1840's must have looked very much the way it had when the first little Spanish ships sailed timidly along it. Possibly the only difference was that now, carrion buzzards were not perched on the gaunt limbs of mangrove trees, but on the rooftops of the squalid

47

and unhappy little towns—Portobelo, Nombre de Dios, and San Lorenzo in Limon Bay.

Unlike their Spanish predecessors, these gold seekers were landed from the ships without benefit of medieval fanfare or panoply. When the surf was high they were unceremoniously dumped from lighters into the water itself!

Conditions ashore were chaotic. The principal port was San Lorenzo, and it was a scene of "unbelievable confusion and iniquity." Through the filthy muddy streets of the old gold port, men staggered, fought, cursed, crowded the saloons and gambling houses. Red-shirted '49ers were everywhere, and they all had but one thought: get across the Isthmus as soon as possible and on to California.

Highwaymen, gunmen, gamblers, prostitutes—adventurers of all descriptions flocked to Panama and reaped a rich harvest preying on the transients. As fast as one shipload was fleeced and got away across the Isthmus, fresh victims arrived. Only the human vultures remained behind to await the new arrivals. In addition to the man-made miseries, the miners were also scourged by malaria, cholera, typhoid, deadly dysenteries, yellow fever and other assorted lethal maladies.

There was but one way out of the rip-roaring city of San Lorenzo: in canoes up the Chagres to where it crossed the old Las Cruces Trail, and then down to Panama City. Once again the dim jungle tunnel was crowded with hurrying and desperate men. Sullen Indians, with a built-in grudge against all white men, got rich ferrying the frantic Yankees up the river to the trail.

In Panama City the transients found things no better.

Ships to San Francisco were far and few between, and so the miserable human flood piled up here in another log jam.

Something had to give. The changes that took place were sparked initially by, of all things, the United States Post Office! Some new way had to be found to carry the growing volume of mail from the East Coast to California, and the Panama route was logical. Contracts were let and soon a small fleet of paddle steamers was chuffing back and forth between New York and Limon Bay on one side and Panama City and San Francisco on the other. The ships in the Pacific helped to relieve the congestion on that side, but it was more than offset by the number of new arrivals at San Lorenzo, for of course in addition to mail, the ships carried passengers.

The tremendous bottleneck, both for mail and for people was that ghastly fifty-mile hike through the jungle. A railroad was the obvious answer. Three enterprising men—William Aspinwall, John L. Stephen and Henry Chauncey—incorporated the Panama Railroad Company in New York and secured a concession from New Granada.

They decided the road could be built in six months at a cost of one million dollars. True, there were swamps, but these could be filled. Crews of men could chop through the jungle and the numerous rivers and streams could easily be bridged. The cordillera, or hump, rose to a modest 300 feet— no height to deter railroad men who were already eyeing the Rockies and Sierra Nevada. To lay several miles of rail a day was commonplace in the States, and so the estimated time and money seemed reasonable for this little bit of track which seemed scarcely more than an oversized spur.

They should have consulted the ghosts who haunted the ancient trails!

The jumping-off place was to be near the old fort of San Lorenzo. Good solid ground extended about twenty-five miles inland, and presumably it would not be too difficult to run the line up this valley. However, an early real estate shark had leased all the land and was holding out for what seemed an unreasonable price. Very well! In their appalling innocence, the outraged railroad men simply moved a few miles further down the bay and selected another spot—a low bit of land called Manzanillo Island. Here they made their headquarters.

From the very beginning, the Isthmus fought the new invaders. Men and equipment started inland and were promptly swallowed up in mud. Nobody seemed to have noticed the swamps that lay between the island and the distant solid mountains. For many months the company was unable even to set up quarters on the little gridiron of streets which had been surveyed on the island. Soapy, slippery, gummy, bottomless, obscured in miasmic vapors and swirling clouds of insects, the swamps waited. The laborers vanished at dawn in the rowboats from the ships into the drenching rains, the steaming muck and gumbo. They labored all day like lost and forgotten slaves. Up to their necks in mud, they stumbled, slipped, struggled and cursed. Over their heads black clouds of mosquitoes and other insects whined and buzzed. They emerged at night soaked to the skin and caked with mud, to fall more dead than alive into the boats, and were taken out to where a grimy brig and the paddle steamer *Telegraph* rolled in the long gray swells.

Thousands upon thousands of tons of fill were swallowed like grains of sand. In some places pilings were driven into the mess and the wobbly roadbed was built on top of them.

In other places, no solid bottom could be found as deep down as 180 feet. The few feet of track so painfully laid each day was often gone, sunk, vanished forever by next morning.

Sickness took such a terrible toll that the men could work only one week out of three. The company was bedeviled from the start by the problem of manpower. High wages lured gangs of husky Irish immigrants to the job, but their brawn was no match for the heat, the rain and the fevers. Then a thousand Chinese laborers were imported. Of these, only two hundred survived. The rest died of fevers, wandered off or committed suicide. Convinced that somewhere there must be a happier place than this hell to which they had been enticed, they joined hands and walked into the sea, sat on rocks and waited for the tide to wash over them, or hung themselves by their queues.

In the end, the company discovered that for heavy work in the tropics, no race of men could match West Indian Negroes. Slow-moving, accustomed to heat, resistant to the fevers, these cheerful and humble people played a most honorable part in the realization of man's dreams on the Isthmus.

At the end of *twenty months,* by toil and sweat and back-break, *seven* precarious miles of track had been laid. The ends of the rails lay on reasonably solid ground at Gatun, on the edge of the Chagres Valley. Work came to a halt. The money was all gone and the backers could not understand how it could take *anyone,* no matter how lazy or what the difficulties, so long to build a measly seven miles of railroad.

A trick of nature saved the project. Two big paddle-wheel steamers, the *Georgia* and the *Philadelphia,* arrived in the bay carrying more than a thousand gold-hungry men. A hurricane roared in from the sea and the ships took refuge behind nearby Manzanillo Island. Imagine the astonishment when the passengers found a railroad ready-made to whisk them across the Isthmus.

The road builders were appalled at the prospect of their pitiful facilities being overwhelmed by such a mob of men—most of them armed and in a big hurry. They protested that their road was only seven miles long and came to an abrupt stop in an impassable jungle. Who cared! Seven miles were seven miles. The '49ers would handle the jungle when they got to it. Frantic to get rid of the mob, the trainmen set fares which were sky-high—$25.00 to ride seven miles and $10.00 to walk the right of way. It seemed a bargain to the Yankees who piled aboard the work trains and were on their way.

From then on San Lorenzo was doomed. The bonanza for the Indians who operated the canoes was over. All ships discharged at Manzanillo Island. The human vultures in San Lorenzo simply moved to the island and took up business there.

In New York the effect of this initial thousand passengers was electric. Despite its puny length, the railroad was a success. More money was raised and the work continued. Slowly and painfully the tracks wormed their way across rivers, through the jungles and over the mountains.

The Panama Railroad is possibly the only line in the world that literally lifted itself up by its own shoelaces. All during the gold rush, miners were taken as far as the end of the road and then continued the journey on foot. The same high fares were in existence for years. Why reduce them? The passengers never complained! By the time the road was finished, nearly a third of its tremendous cost had already been liquidated.

At long last, during a torrential rainstorm, the final spikes on the road were driven in Panama City at midnight on January 27, 1855. The next morning a locomotive made the run from the Atlantic to the Pacific for the first time in history.

Old-timers claim that each tie in the road cost a human life. Like all old-timers' tales, this is somewhat overdone, as there are more than 80,000 ties. Actually the toll was fearsome, and needs no exaggeration. Of the 6,000 men who worked on the railroad, 835 are known to have perished on the job. No one knows how many perished from sickness, suicide and other causes.

Instead of the planned six months and one million dollars cost, the road had taken five years and seven million dollars. Its construction ranks with man's greatest triumphs of engineering and human determination. It is a wonder it was ever completed, and had it not been for that lucky hurricane, it very well might not have been. The number of bridges which had to be built was fantastic. The road was 47 miles long, and 147 bridges had been built. Some of them were small structures, but others, like that which crossed the Chagres at Barbacoas, were tremendous. Many disastrous attempts were made before the engineers realized that during a heavy downpour, this river could rise 25 feet in 24 hours. Bridges had to be so strong, they could withhold the tremendous force of the water.

For years after its completion, the Panama Railroad was an even greater success than it had been during its construction. It earned almost twelve million dollars *net* during the first ten years of operation. For many years its stock was regarded as one of the world's best and safest investments—understandable as yearly dividends topped 24 per cent!

During Spanish colonial days, the quick source of money had been the Indian mines, the pearl fisheries, the graves. During the early days of the railroad, it had been the urgent traffic to California. However, during each boom, the true destiny of this "narrow place between the seas" became apparent.

The Spaniards enjoyed a brisk trade in goods bound for the far ports of the Pacific and transshipped over the old trails. The Panama Railroad too, found rich sources of revenue other than those brought by the gold rush.

The road enjoyed a real monopoly on all heavy transportation between the East and West coasts of North America and South America as well. In addition, many European shipping lines found it easier and cheaper to transship goods across the Isthmus than to go all the way around Cape Horn.

The Pacific Steam Navigation Company, a large British firm, was a good example. Their trade was mainly between Europe and Australia and ports of the far-distant Orient. When the railroad first opened, the company made a few trial shipments and found this new route between the Atlantic and Pacific so satisfactory that it decided to set up permanent installations on the Isthmus. Freight sheds, cargo-handling equipment and larger docks at both terminals of the road, so as to further speed up and facilitate their operations, were built. On Taboga, a lovely non-malarial island in the middle of Panama Bay, living quarters, offices, warehouses, drydocks and machine shops were erected. The

owners of the Panama Railroad congratulated themselves
that the P.S.N. was in to stay.

When the gold rush was over, income from such sources
as this was steady and lucrative for the railroad. However,
the bubble burst almost overnight.

In 1867, the Panama road's owners negotiated a new concession with the government of New Granada. To be in effect
for ninety-nine years, it gave New Granada $1 million out-
right and guaranteed payments of $250,000 per year. At the
same time as this ruinous financial agreement was completed,
the arrogance of the board of directors landed them in a
terrible row with their best customer—the Pacific Steam
Navigation Company. When the squabble was over, the
steamship people closed up their entire operation and departed in a huff. The news of these developments caused the
railroad stock to tumble from $200 a share to $80 in New
York.

Revenues declined badly, and Panama once again slowly
sank back into its somnolence. By 1870 all the big profits
were gone for the road. Just as with Las Cruces Trail when
it had been abandoned, so the railroad deteriorated. Soon it
was scarcely more than twin streaks of rust in the encircling
jungle, with infrequent trains and little freight or passenger
business.

Over all these years, the clamor for somebody to cut a
canal across the Isthmus was growing. Far-seeing people
flatly predicted that it was now just a matter of time. The
railroad's concession with New Granada gave it an "exclusive" for all transportation from ocean to ocean. It could pre-
vent anyone from digging a canal along its right of way.

But this did not guarantee that it could block the inevitable for all time.

If anything, the success of the Panama Railroad had stimulated interest in a waterway, and everyone wanted a hand in it. Governments, syndicates and individuals jockeyed frantically for the best positions. All the old surveys were dusted off and re-examined. New ones were undertaken.

The United States, Great Britain and France were most active in all these new explorations. The realization of what a canal would mean was becoming crystal clear to everyone. These new surveys were not just foggy, wild guesses as many of the earlier ones had been. They were thorough, painstaking. In 1866, for example, the United States Navy made a report to the Senate in which nineteen canal and seven road projects were discussed. The report ended with the opinion that "it is to the Isthmus of Darien that we are to look for the solution of the great problem of an interoceanic canal." The "Isthmus of Darien" meant, of course, that part of the Isthmus which is now the country of Panama.

The fortunes of the twin streaks of rust continued to sink lower and lower. Railroads at home had by now spanned the continent and cut ever more deeply into already fast-diminishing sources of revenue. There was further competition from a New York syndicate headed by the old railroad man Commodore Vanderbilt. This syndicate operated a combined ferry and stagecoach route across Nicaragua. Had it not been for local traffic and for the transshipment of small amounts of "feeder" coffee cargoes, the goose which had laid so many rich golden eggs might have turned up its toes and died, just as the mighty empire of Spain had done when its great days were over.

The railroad was luckier than the Spanish had been. In 1881 a new customer appeared, burning with ambition, its pockets bulging with money. To the harassed owners of the road it came over the horizon of the Caribbean like a gift from heaven, ready and able to bail the dying company with its faltering collection of rusty tracks and steam-spurting locomotives out of all its difficulties. This saviour was France.

Chapter 5

The pageant of man's affairs is like a drama. Although we seldom realize it at the time, nothing can take place unless it has been set up perfectly and precisely by the preceding scenes.

Such was the case with the Panama Canal. It had been dreamed about and talked about for centuries. Now it needed to be built, and what's more important, it could be built. Everyone who had tried up to that time failed because picks, shovels and bare hands were not enough. By 1881, however, man's knowledge and skills had increased. He had invented new machinery, he had learned enough about earth moving, dredging, blasting and all the techniques of surveying to make a serious effort.

The nations of the world eyed that Isthmus in the Western Hemisphere a bit uneasily. Warily they pondered. What would such a job *really* be like? No one knew the answer to this.

Quite simply, all that was needed was a man determined enough to take the bull by the horns. He would have to be a man with lots of knowledge, of course, but he would also need something more. He would need a kind of blind confidence in his own destiny, a blind arrogance that would listen to no voice but his own.

Such a man now arrived in Panama. His name was Count Ferdinand de Lesseps. He was perfectly fitted for the role he was to assume. De Lesseps was the man who had built the Suez Canal.

When the Turks in 1453 closed the ancient Silk Roads and other desert routes, the trade between East and West was seriously hurt. When Vasco da Gama rounded the Cape of Good Hope and sea-borne commerce began between Europe and the Orient, the blow to the old trading centers was fatal.

The effort which these once great Mediterranean powers made to pull themselves together and to restore their prestige became an obsession. Over the long years many, many projects were advanced to stimulate trade, but four centuries passed before they were freed from the blind alley in which geography and history had confined them.

Well-built waterways, more than ample in size to carry the largest ships of the day, had been in existence across the Isthmus of Suez in the days of the Pharaohs. Why these ancient, magnificent projects had been allowed to silt up and be filled with drifting sand remains another of the unsolved mysteries of those far-gone days.

The Venetians and the Genoese urged that this old canal be reopened, or even that a new one be dug across the 100-mile Isthmus. The Turks tried to organize and build a great commercial highway across deserts and mountains. The schemes were many, but none of them succeeded. Even the Vatican had a finger in the enterprise when Pope Sixtus V tried to organize a route on the grounds that it would shorten the voyages of his missionaries.

As the peoples of the Near East struggled to find a way out of their dilemma, other events in Europe had been moving swiftly. The matter became political, as well as commercial. With the expansion of vast colonial empires, England and France soon stood glaring at each other across the sands of Suez.

In the late 1700's, Talleyrand, a wily old French statesman, knew what he was talking about when he said: "Opening up the Suez route will react on England in the same way that the discovery of the Cape of Good Hope ruined Genoa and Venice in the sixteenth century. If France is in possession of the Suez route, it matters little into whose hands the Cape of Good Hope may fall." In this one crystal-clear fragment of thought, he set the scene for France and disposed of his arch-enemy—the British Empire.

Napoleon's expedition to Egypt in 1798 had this in mind. His instructions read: "The Army of the Orient shall take possession of Egypt. The Commander-in-Chief shall chase the English from their possessions in the Orient, which he can reach. . . . He shall have the Isthmus of Suez cut through. . . ."

Napoleon and his staff explored the Isthmus thoroughly, including the remains of the ancient canal—a long, desolate ditch empty but for the swirling sand. Napoleon was much too cagey to try to "cut the Isthmus through," but he did instruct his chief engineer, La Pere, to make a most complete survey.

England eventually retaliated by building a railroad— just as had been done at Panama—across the Isthmus. For a time trains made regular connections with ships and chugged their way across the burning sands and rocks between the Mediterranean and Red seas.

France continued to make surveys on the Isthmus and invariably reached the conclusion that a canal could, and should, be built. The old nationalism of Talleyrand had died. In its place was a deep spirit of liberalism, of humanitarianism. The dream of the French government and people was that such a canal should be European, universal, open to all comers and operated for the benefit of all mankind. It should not even be fortified.

In this spirit Ferdinand de Lesseps debarked at Alexandria in 1854. In his head were romantic ideals which were to be for the good of all humanity, but his hopes and dreams were also highly practical and far-seeing. In his pocket he carried a good, sound plan for the digging of the canal, which he wished to present to the viceroy of Egypt.

De Lesseps was responsible for the construction of the Suez Canal and the consequent creation of an entirely new trade route on our earth. It was a route which profoundly altered the politics of the world, its geography and the way of life of millions of people.

Yet de Lesseps was not an engineer; he was not a construction man in any sense of the word. He was not even an administrator. He was a visionary, a man with ideals, whose faith in himself and in his dreams was so great that he enthused everyone around him, enabling him to accomplish miracles. He was also a very honest man, with little interest in acquiring a huge fortune for himself. This disinterest was certainly a part of the great appeal he had for people.

De Lesseps had spent his younger years in the French diplomatic service, for the most part at Eastern posts. He was completely at home in an Oriental atmosphere and was deeply mystic. In strange contrast to this side of his nature, he was also a man of incredible energy, bursting with enthusiasm and with a desire to get things done in a hurry. These qualities made him the man perfectly suited for the successful construction of the Suez Canal—a vast project in an Oriental land, involving a minimum of engineering difficulties.

In keeping with the spirit of France at this time, de Lesseps planned that the Canal would not be controlled by any government. It was to be built and run by a private enterprise, for profit, of course, and for the good of all. He planned that ownership would be about 15 per cent government, 10 per cent among the founders and instigators of the scheme and 75 per cent among private investors. As it worked out, much of the money came from the small savings of French middle- and lower-class people who were successfully wooed through de Lesseps' knowledge of psychology and mass propaganda. These people hoped to turn an honest *centime* or two and, at the same time in true Gallic style, strike a resounding blow for the ideals and prestige of *La Belle France*.

About ten years were necessary for the digging of the waterway. During this time de Lesseps moved through a nightmare of intrigue—financial, political, domestic, European and Oriental. At times matters became so complicated that the digging actually ground to a halt. Agonizingly short of money, de Lesseps knew exactly how to make the right appeal to the French people. Toward the end, disaster was averted only by a gigantic public lottery, in which Suez Canal bonds were the prizes.

As de Lesseps threaded his way, nimble and sure-footed

as a cat, the Canal inched its way over the desert. There were many problems, of course, but in general they were relatively easy to solve. Such things as ditches to bring fresh water from the Nile, living quarters and camps for laborers, sanitation facilities and the placing of tidal gates were the stumbling blocks rather than real problems demanding a high degree of modern engineering skill. The highest elevation between the Mediterranean and Red seas was a mere sixty feet. Most of the ground was so sandy that a great deal of the work was accomplished by light dredges and in many instances by scoops, shovels or even the bare hands of the thousands of *fellahin*, the native Egyptian laborers.

When the great job was completed, de Lesseps was a world-wide hero. In France he was revered as the man who had provided tens of thousands of French families with a tidy little investment and at the same time had demonstrated the greatness of the nation. In France and elsewhere he was commonly and most affectionately known as the "Great Frenchman."

The completion of the Suez Canal demonstrated that such titanic projects were well within man's capabilities. One more great canal still remained to be cut, and eyes all over the world began to turn in cool speculation to the Western Hemisphere, to the Isthmus which joined the two Americas.

In 1872 the Congress of the United States had created an Interoceanic Canal Commission with orders to study the whole problem of a canal to connect the Pacific and Atlantic oceans. Four years later this body submitted its report. Overwhelmingly the august members recommended a route across Nicaragua.

A distinguished group in Europe—mostly French—had

also formed to consider the same problem. Quite logically, de Lesseps was a member. These people examined the route through Nicaragua as proposed by the Americans. They found it unsatisfactory and turned their attention to the Isthmus of Panama.

After a very perfunctory survey, an optimistic and rosy report was turned in, adopted, and the French lost no time entering into negotiations with the Republic of Colombia, which had split off from the old Bolivarian entity of New Granada. France received a concession.

The next problem was to choose a director and de Lesseps was, of course, the most natural choice. His family, however, and his most intimate friends were dubious. This new venture was an unknown quantity. By now he had money and fame enough for any man. There were too many disquieting rumors about the ugly reputation of the Isthmus of Panama.

De Lesseps' thirty-eight-year-old son Charles, who had been a staunch supporter during the trying days at Suez, was strongly opposed. He told his father: "You have earned enough glory. Why not leave this to someone else? Think of the risk. Your success in Suez was a miracle. Be content with one miracle in your lifetime and do not hope for a second."

De Lesseps, at this time, was a man of seventy-four years, but he was vital and vigorous. He was vain, too, and he loved popularity and action and movement. Naturally he was enormously flattered by the offer and sorely tempted.

Again Charles argued and when he realized nothing would make his father change his mind, he said: "Should you wish me to join you I shall do so with the best will in the world. I shall not complain no matter what happens. All that I am

I owe to you. What you have given me you have the right to take away."

De Lesseps accepted the task. The road into the future was wide open and irresistibly called to his romantic heart.

Amidst great ceremony the *Compagnie Universelle du Canal Interoceanique du Panama* was organized. The cost of the Canal was estimated at 1,174 million francs, or about $214 million. Of the seventy-eight members of the advisory board who so enthusiastically fixed this great sum, twenty were engineers and only one of them had ever set foot in Panama!

Next, and quite properly, de Lesseps had to examine the scene of the future canal with his own eyes. Full of confidence and joy, this extraordinary old man sailed for the Isthmus and arrived there early in 1880. A team of international engineering experts accompanied him. In the party also were his pretty young wife and his three small children—the latter possibly to prove that the stories about Panama's dangerous climate were only nasty and unfounded rumors spread by jealous adversaries of the scheme!

Mademoiselle Fernande de Lesseps made a charming picture as she stood on the deck of the tugboat *Taboguilla*. Her dainty white dress was starched and lacy; her white umbrella, which she held over her head, framed her fresh and piquant face. In her free hand she held a small, decorated pickax, with which she was to inaugurate the work on the Panama Canal. An elegant and distinguished company, including her aged father, was gathered on the deck about her.

The *Taboguilla* slid smoothly over the sparkling blue water to a small inlet in Panama Bay—the mouth of the Rio

Grande River. No one seemed to remember that the tides on the Pacific side of the Isthmus rise and fall upward from eighteen feet! When the puffing tugboat arrived at the inlet, the water was all drained from it, and there was nothing but a vast, sloppy tidal flat. The boat very narrowly escaped being stranded high and dry.

What was the party to do? After a good deal of pleasant conversation and the steady popping of champagne corks, a young member of the committee was inspired to action. Beautiful clothes and all, he leaped overboard to the accompaniment of spirited clapping for his gallantry and hoisted back on the tugbot a box of gooey, soapy mud.

Mademoiselle Fernande sank the point of her tiny pickax into the muck. She was followed by other distinguished people present. The pretty ceremony was capped by a few graceful words from her father. The Bishop of Panama blessed the assemblage and the work to be done, and the *Taboguilla* returned to the dock.

Some time later, high on the slopes of the continental divide in the interior, Mademoiselle de Lesseps pressed a button which was supposed to explode a charge of dynamite, but nothing happened. There was no sound other than the popping of champagne corks.

Technicians scurried about trying to find out what was wrong. Finally the proper contact was made, and the dynamite let go with a roar most satisfying to the Gallic and Latin hearts gathered for the show.

The Isthmus put on a triumphal celebration which lasted six weeks. Nightly fireworks splashed the velvet tropic sky. Fiesta followed fiesta. Plays, tableaus, receptions and great public demonstrations followed hard upon each other. De

Lesseps was the hero of the hour, and he was indefatigable. After nights of celebration and dancing, he awoke each morning fresh and energetic and rode the steep trails and mountains along the proposed route of the Canal like a twenty-year-old.

Occasionally questions were put to him about such things as exact surveys, drainage, cubic yards of excavation anticipated and the like. De Lesseps had one answer. "The Canal will be built," he airily replied.

"The Canal will be built," he affirmed, and remembering Suez, people believed. As happened with Columbus long before him who had believed so devoutly in the presence of the water route to Cathay that his faith rubbed off on the rest of the world, so did de Lesseps' faith rub off on his listeners. "The Canal will be built." So it would be. Meantime the fireworks burst, more champagne was consumed and speeches were made. Budgets were blithly trimmed or expanded and all was well.

When the triumphant six weeks were over, sterner tasks had to be tackled. The first one was to placate the United States, where opposition to the French plans was mounting.

Prominent American capitalists and engineers had organized to construct the Nicaraguan Canal and were actually far beyond the mere planning stage. De Lesseps realized he must stop them at all costs. There could not obviously, be profits enough to support *two* canals.

He set aside a very sizable block of shares in the Canal for American subscription and left for the United States. The charming Frenchman and his family were treated royally by the American people and by the government, but on practical matters, there was much coolness.

American capital was reluctant to take advantage of the generous offer to invest. In spite of de Lesseps' glowing talk about the grandeur of the project and of how the Canal was destined to be open and useful to all of mankind, President Hayes doggedly stuck to his belief that the Canal should be American. He sent a message to the Senate in which he stated that any such waterway should be controlled by the United States and that we should not in any way surrender such control to any European group.

De Lesseps set about making his point by more indirect methods. An office was opened in New York. Large sums of money were deposited in banks there. He was a master of the art of propaganda and free with his money. Some two million dollars later the subsidized newspaper campaigns had their effect.

Public opinion was influenced in favor of the French. The policy as advised by President Hayes and the Nicaraguan route as well were effectively blocked.

Back home in France, a triumphant de Lesseps faced another practical problem—money to build the Canal. At this stage, there *was* no problem. He made a whirlwind speaking and lecture tour and the initial sum required, sixty million dollars, was far oversubscribed.

So great was the faith of the common people of France in their Great Frenchman, that he could do no wrong. Had not the conqueror of Suez stated that the Panama Canal "will be built"? Didn't he add, by way of reassurance, that since the Panama Canal was only half as long as that at Suez, it would take only half as long to build and cost half as much?

Most of this great sum of sixty million dollars came from

middle-class people, who could buy only one to five shares. The tin cans, the stockings and the sugar bowls were turned upside down. The first of what was eventually estimated to be the savings of half a million French families poured out in a golden flood.

The Great Frenchman was on his way.

Waiting for him was the Isthmus of Panama . . . with all its whispering ghosts.

Chapter 6

Some miles above the town of Colon—as the city which the railroad engineers had so laboriously laid out on Manzanillo Island came to be called—there is a low rise in the earth. The original name of this rise was Monkey Hill, named after the huge tribes of chattering monkeys which frolicked through its trees.

Shortly after the French started work, the name Monkey Hill was changed to Mt. Hope, for an equally appropriate reason. On Mt. Hope was located the largest of many cemeteries on the Isthmus.

By 1888, seven or eight years later, another name was changed—that of de Lesseps, the Great Frenchman. As Mt. Hope and other burial grounds began to bulge, he came to be know as the "Great Undertaker."

Death was not new to the Isthmus. Since earliest times its trails and swamps and rivers ran red with blood—Indian, Spanish, English, Scotch, Dutch, Irish, Chinese, Negro and many others. The greedy specters which stalked the mists over the mountains and swamps and forests of Panama had never seen anything like what was going on now.

No one really knows what the total loss of life was during the French period in Panama. As nearly as can be estimated from old hospital records, and counts in the cemeteries, about two thousand French engineers and administrative officials gave their lives, plus another twenty thousand laborers, mostly West Indian Negroes and others native to nearby countries.

It was easy to laugh at the pompous, vain and foolishly idealistic de Lesseps; to sneer at the graft and corruption and waste which went on; to frown upon the riot of drinking and debauchery and gambling which almost immediately arose in the old French towns on the Isthmus! But there was little heart for sneering or laughter as one walked through the old cemeteries.

Those French names on the stones were the names of men who died young, for an ideal. Few of them were over twenty-five. Year after year young men came across the sea, even after the name Panama became synonymous with death. Two out of three of the French who came to the Isthmus perished but there was never any lack of recruits.

They died miserably and pitifully. They were not heroes who met death in clashing battle, with racing blood and flashing steel. They died of yellow fever and malaria. They died in a struggle with an enemy which science had not yet equipped them to combat.

Very early the French realized that something was terribly wrong with their medical facilities. Accordingly, they built hospitals—fine hospitals with all the latest equipment and surrounded by beautiful shrubs and gardens.

To protect the patients from ants, the legs of the beds were placed in little pans of water. The ants were effectively halted, but had the doctors wished deliberately to spread the horrible fevers from bed to bed they could not have done better. Very soon the little pans were filled with wrigglers which hatched into malarial mosquitoes.

The beautiful shrubbery and gardens outside the broad open windows and verandas provided perfect nesting places for yellow fever mosquitoes, who need shade in which to breed. These mosquitoes could not fly a hundred yards in bright sunlight and live, but the dense vegetation gave them just what they needed to multiply.

These were not deliberate or callous mistakes of the French, or the French doctors. They just didn't know what caused these diseases. It wasn't until years later when brave men volunteered to be bitten by mosquitoes, that the true facts about yellow fever became known.

In the face of such constant death, it is not strange that men were apt to be careless and extravagant in their pleasures. So it was on the Isthmus during these years. The towns ran riot. The drinking, the gambling, the dancing . . . and the dying . . . never stopped. "Today we live because tomorrow we die" seemed to be the credo by which men lived.

At the same time there was an unceasing orgy of graft and corruption which spread clear back to France. Money was spent lavishly; it flowed as freely as the champagne. Tremendous salaries were paid; payrolls were padded beyond belief. Supplies flowed from Europe in a steady river and much of them seemed to have been shipped with no other purpose than to make a fat profit for the suppliers.

Once on the Isthmus, a great deal of the equipment and machinery was allowed to rust, to sink into the mud, to be dumped into swamps to form foundations for buildings which were never used and which in their turn sank despairingly into the muck and vanished. Shiploads of cement were stacked outdoors in the rain, and soon hardened into great pyramids, mute tombstones to a dying venture. A small flotilla of iron steamboats was laboriously hauled overland up into the mountains near the great cuts, for the day when they would sail triumphantly out to sea. Meantime they slowly melted down into blobs of rust, great mounds mercifully hidden by the jungle. Fifteen thousand kerosene torches, specially shipped for the jubilant completion ceremonies, took space in sagging warehouses. A thousand snow shovels—maybe somebody thought a canal could be dug with them—placidly added their own piles of rust.

Jules Dingler, one of France's greatest construction men, was the first chief engineer on the project. He would be satisfied with nothing less than a fine Victorian mansion for a residence. It cost $150,000, including stables for the horses which he and his family loved to ride. The bath house alone ran to $40,000, while his private railroad car cost $42,000. "Dingler's Folly" all this came to be called, and indeed it was folly. His wife, his son and his daughter died of yellow fever. He took their favorite horses up into the hills, shot the animals, then returned to France where he died, insane, of a broken heart.

The appalling confusion, the ignorance and the lack of preparation of the French as they got into their monumental task was apparent in a thousand ways—particularly during the early periods. For example, the twin streaks of rust—the Panama Railroad—had exclusive rights for all transit of any kind across the Isthmus. Unbelievably, the French entered into no discussions with the owners of the railroad to clarify their relations.

As the ships began to arrive in Limon Bay, thousands upon

thousands of tons of supplies and machinery piled up. The gold rush had been nothing compared to this fat bonanza for the Panama Railroad. Belatedly, de Lesseps' representatives brought up the question of rates. To their horror, they found the directors of the road would consider no concessions. The old tariffs—the highest the world has ever known —were to remain in effect.

Such outrageous costs would have broken the French before they even started to dig, and so they elected to buy the road outright. Joyously the stockholders prepared to unload. The negotiators "generously" paid $250 a share—a total of $25 million for 68/70 of the stock—even though the going price was only $70 a share. A few American shareholders had their eyes on bigger profits and refused to sell. By court injunction they kept their places on the board of directors; and the road remained under American management and retained its identity as an American enterprise incorporated in New York, even though almost totally owned by the French!

During the French "occupation," the waste was incredible, staggering, senseless. That the whole project went on as long as it did is tribute to the pompous but determined little man in Paris, Ferdinand de Lesseps. "The Canal will be built," he said, and people believed him.

Meantime, quite unbelievably, the Canal *was being built*. Far up in the hills, deep in the swamps and over vast grassy plains, the painful work of scratching a ditch from ocean to ocean continued. As time passed, and in spite of everything, the work progressed. Careful maps were made; plans were drawn. Entry channels to the sea were dredged. Railroads were built. Dump grounds, to which the "spoil" was carried, were established. Enormous amounts of earth—about 60 million cubic yards—were excavated, and the continental divide was lowered by 161 feet. After heartbreaking trials and errors, proper machinery was designed, ordered and used to good effect.

The technical and engineering feats of the French were good. Their efforts were heroic. Very possibly they might have finished the job if the administrative staff had been as good as the engineering.

At de Lesseps' insistence, and against the advice of many of his engineers, it was to be a sea-level canal. In other words, the cuts were to be made right straight down until there was an uninterrupted path of water from one ocean to the other. Gates and basins were to be installed on the Pacific side to take care of the great rise and fall of the tides. Part of the canal was to follow the bed of the Chagres River—that most undependable of all streams. It could turn from a tranquil creek into a raging torrent almost overnight. The engineers sought to lick this by building diversion channels and control dams, but the work was expensive and took a great deal of time.

Another problem was the cut through the cordillera. It was 300 feet high, and this meant, of course, that a cut over 300 feet deep would have to be made to get down to sea level. The earth in these mountains was not ordinary earth. It was composed principally of two kinds of soil, in flat layers, held together by streaks of clay. When wet or disturbed, this clay caused the layers of rock and soil to slip and slide as though they were greased. As fast as it was dug out, enormous masses of earth were continuously dislodged, pouring and flowing down over work already done and burying it and equipment deep in mud. The deeper they went, the worse these slides became.

Before many years had passed, competent engineers realized that with the time and money allotted, a sea-level canal might never be finished. Accordingly, they started agitating for a change in plans. They said, quite reasonably, that a high-level, lock waterway could be completed quickly, and the company could start collecting tolls. After the Canal was in operation, they proposed to continue by dredging, starting at the highest level and eventually cutting right down to sea level. If these sensible and practical men had been allowed to go through with this idea, the story might have had a different ending. De Lesseps, however, refused to consider such a thing. His judgment was at stake!

By 1887 affairs were in such desperate shape that even he was willing to consider anything that would permit the work to go on. Plans were hurriedly drawn for a lock canal . . . but there was no more money.

In Paris as well as on the Isthmus, graft and corruption had reached staggering proportions. The whole organization was shot through with rascally politicians, crooked journalists, blackmailers. All of them had itchy palms deep in the till.

Public confidence in the Great Frenchman was gone. Vainly the Great Undertaker appealed for faith. He tried everything he could think of to raise funds: change of plans, new stock issues, reorganization, appeals to the government for help. There was no use. The deaths, the inefficiency, the vast sums which had already vanished across the ocean so uselessly, had done their work. People were beginning to realize that the Panama Canal would never be a goose that laid eggs as golden as those at Suez.

When de Lesseps finally gave permission for a lock canal to be built, he petitioned the French government for permission to raise money by conducting a lottery. The permission was granted. This maneuver had furnished the capital which saved the Suez Canal during its black days, and de Lesseps had high hopes now. Tirelessly he toured the country making speeches and trying to whip up enthusiasm.

The people had had enough. The attempt was useless. Of the $160 million hoped for, only a tenth was collected. Additional inducements proved futile. Sadly de Lesseps returned this small amount and telegraphed the Isthmus that work was to stop.

On December 14, 1888, the company went into receivership and the bubble burst. The fires were drawn from the boilers, the machinery left to the mercy of the jungle. Thousands of persons were left stranded—there wasn't enough money to get them home. The government of Jamaica sent ships to repatriate 6,000 Negroes who were starving. Chile offered 40,000 free passages from Panama, and for months ships sailing southward carried their quotas of ex-employees seeking places to start new lives.

Over a *quarter of a billion dollars* had been poured into the great Panama dream—and all of it had vanished. For a short time the magnitude of the disaster stunned France. The savings of half the middle class of the nation were gone. At first people were shocked, reluctant to face the truth. And then the clamor began. There must be an investigation. Who was responsible? Where had the money gone and why?

De Lesseps at this time was a spry eighty-three. Age had

not yet dimmed his enormous vitality. However, on that fateful day when he ordered work stopped on the Isthmus, it was as though he had suffered a stroke. Though he lived for another five years, it was only as a shadow playing a part in the epilogue of a bitter tragedy.

In the investigation which followed, the scandal that was aired was past belief. When the affairs of the company were brought out in open court, a horrified world learned the whole sorry story. In addition to mismanagement, it was learned that over one hundred French senators and deputies had taken bribes. Five former cabinet ministers were brought to trial along with the directors of the company. The financial agent, who had done most of the bribing, committed suicide. Two other high officials fled the country.

De Lesseps and his ever-loyal son Charles were sentenced to five years imprisonment and ordered to pay a heavy fine. The ferocity of the investigation and the punishments were finally blunted and revoked, however. Corruption and graft and misrepresentation all had taken place, but no criminal action by father or son was ever proved. They were completely honest and had conducted themselves with great probity. They were above reproach in this respect. Innocent, lacking in wisdom, duped by unscrupulous associates—yes. Dishonest, attempting to defraud—no.

De Lesseps had been a superb fighter, with more faith in his own destiny than in hard, cold analysis of a situation. Faith had done the job for him in Suez, but the very qualities which had enabled him to succeed there had defeated him in Panama. At Suez, where engineering skill had been less important, faith, deep mysticism and dogged determination had been enough. In Panama, all these qualities might have been equally important, but they had to be coupled with superb medical and engineering skills—and here he failed.

To the ghosts who walk the Isthmus were now added thousands of new ones. They watched and waited to see who would be the next visitor to their festering strip of earth.

They didn't have long to wait.

Chapter 7

In the heart of Panama City, long shadows fell across the flowers and grass in the little park of Cathedral Plaza. In the flame trees and through the gaudy bougainvillea, blue and green parakeets and a pair of tiny monkeys protested the coming of the day.

Mark Brooke, Second Lieutenant in the Corp of Engineers, United States Army, strode briskly through a large and elegantly dressed crowd gathered in front of the huge headquarters building of the French Canal Company. For the occasion, Lieutenant Brooke had put on his nattiest white dress uniform.

He entered the building and was greeted courteously by the manager and assembled employees. A few moments later Brooke scratched his name on some documents, and the people of the United States became owners—lock, stock and barrel—of all French properties and equipment on the Isthmus of Panama.

The lieutenant had composed a few words which he considered appropriate. He now read them off, and departed.

The crowd of onlookers was disappointed. The Panamanian and French officials gathered in the plaza had hoped for something a bit more impressive. Some champagne perhaps, or at least a few marching troops with rolling drums, or some fireworks were certainly in order. There had been nothing—only Lieutenant Brooke! Everyone conceded that the French knew how to do this sort of thing better and agreed glumly that the *Norteamericanos* were a pretty unemotional lot.

Between the time of the bursting of the French dream in 1888, and this simple ceremony on May 4, 1904, a very great deal had taken place. There had been enough excitement to satisfy anyone. Perhaps Lieutenant Brooke, even though he had worn his dress whites, was simply anticlimactic. For sixteen years an incredibly complex drama of cloak and dagger had unfolded. Some of the acts were so well shrouded in mystery that we can't ever know what really took place. We can only look at the results and guess.

The curtain rose on the drama in Paris. While the public howled that the directors of the French Canal project be brought to justice, others took a more down-to-earth view. Just possibly, they thought, something might be salvaged from the wreckage. The stakes were very high.

Accordingly, a "new" French Canal Company was formed. It was headed by a few wealthy financiers and by Philippe Bunau-Varilla, a most extraordinary person. He was a humanitarian; he was idealistic. He was also extremely intelligent and highly practical. An engineer by profession, he had been associated with de Lesseps both at Suez and in Panama. For a while, even though only twenty-six years old at the time, he had been chief engineer on the Panama job, and he also had a great deal of money invested in the company.

The "liquidators" had much to do. First things first. Men had to be kept at work on the Canal or the concession with

Colombia would lapse. Sixteen million dollars was raised and a token laboring force put on the payroll. They pecked away in the cuts and painted and maintained such equipment as was still serviceable.

Next, the expiration date on the concession with Colombia was set ahead. After several extensions, 1910 was agreed upon. This gave the company some much-needed time in which to maneuver.

Still with faith in the Canal, Bunau-Varilla and associates attempted to raise more money in France to continue the job. The effort was hopeless. Frenchmen had had their fill of Panama. By 1898, the company resolved to try and sell out. In spite of the mess, they had some good, valuable merchandise to sell.

They put a value of $101,141,500 on all of it, and set out to trade. They began a walk on such an amazingly precarious tightrope that it is a wonder they ever reached the other side. That they did is a tribute to Bunau-Varilla's mastery of the dark techniques of intrigue and skulduggery.

In his mind, Bunau-Varilla settled quite logically on the United States as his customer. The young nation was beginning to flex its muscles. The country extended from coast to coast; the war with Spain had been successfully concluded and they now had overseas possessions. Pride in their growing land was rising. Americans realized that they *needed* a canal to bring their two coastlines closer together. This need had been forcefully dramatized during the Spanish-American War. In 1898, the battleship *Oregon*, one of the most powerful fighting ships of the United States Navy, was in the Pacific. In order to join the main fleet, which was operating in Cuban waters, the *Oregon* had to make a desperate, time-consuming dash of nearly thirteen thousand miles around the continent of South America. The implications of this, and the knowledge that the voyage could have been avoided by a fifty-mile ditch, was a lesson learned by the American people and their government.

Many obstacles lay in Bunau-Varilla's path. He tackled them with *elan*, with true Gallic enthusiasm.

Because of many previous surveys, most of America had been sold on the Nicaraguan route—or so it seemed. If Bunau-Varilla was going to salvage anything out of Panama for himself, his country, or even for the thousands of investors in France, he must somehow turn our attention away from Nicaragua.

A firm of New York lawyers—Sullivan and Cromwell—was appointed company representative in the States. They and their employer, Bunau-Varilla, proceeded to bombard the American public and Congress with propaganda. For this purpose Bunau-Varilla sent lengthy cablegrams, daily totaling several hundred dollars.

At times the cause was saved by only a hair. In 1902 the House of Representatives had voted almost unanimously for the Nicaragua route. Nine days later the Senate was to vote. In the meantime Nicaragua foolishly issued a postage stamp on which was engraved a smoking volcano. Bunau-Varilla used this with telling effect. Naturally, a land of volcanoes and earthquakes was no place for a canal! "I will obtain ninety of these precious documents, one for each Senator," he cried. "Meanwhile, my secretary will type on ninety little slips of paper, underneath where the postage stamps will go, the following appropriate words: 'Postage stamp from the Republic of Nicaragua. An official witness of volcanic activity on the Isthmus of Nicaragua!' "

The effect was sure and swift. The American Congress passed what was known as the Spooner Act. It authorized the Panama route, provided the French would sell out for $40 million. The French balked, so the Americans again revived interest in Nicaragua. Under this threat, Bunau-Varilla dropped his sights to meet the offered price.

There was another, very serious barrier. It was necessary to obtain from Colombia the concession for the rights to build a canal. The concession which the French had, could not be transferred to any other country. The Americans sent an ambassador to Bogota and negotiations were opened.

The Colombians balked. They reasoned that if they did nothing, then seven years hence when the French grant expired, presumably the whole thing, including the juicy $40 million, would drop into their laps.

The debate raged in the Colombian Senate. The situation of Egypt and Suez was compared to that of Colombia and Panama. Blindly the country refused to see that the two were not similar. Egypt was practically astride Suez; Colombia's capital and the bulk of her territory were over five hundred miles distant—across the sea or over deadly jungle.

Further, Colombia never had any great love for the "Colossus of the North." Yankees, gringos, were not regarded very highly. Colombia began hinting that negotiations with Germany and, of all things, with Japan were under consideration for the construction of the Canal when the French pulled out.

Something had to be done. Time was very swiftly running out for Bunau-Varilla. Delay was all to Colombia's advantage; to him it would be fatal. What happened next is known. Who pulled the strings is less clear.

The Colombians had closed their eyes to one important facet of the problem. When this was set in motion and exploited by the wily Bunau-Varilla, it turned the tide in his favor.

This possibility was revolt by the people who lived on the Isthmus—the Panamanians. They were restless, seething, resentful of their treatment by Colombia. The province was regarded in Bogota as a kind of awkward and unhappy little stepchild.

Revolt was nothing new on the Isthmus. From 1846 to 1903, the Panamanians had staged no less than fifty-three "riots, rebellions and revolutions." They had all been suppressed by the military, and many of these "incidents" had been horribly bloody and brutal. Some of them were so bad that the Colombian government had called in United States Marines to help put them down. This they had the right to do under the treaty of 1846 if it became necessary to keep order along the route of the Panama Railroad.

By 1903 Panama was again in violent discontent. Another bloody revolution had just been beaten down. The people longed to put an end to this uneasy relationship with a semi-hostile government so far away. They wanted their freedom. In addition, they were sick over the delay of the construction of the Canal. The French had pulled out, and the economic life of the Isthmus was dead. The lottery was in the doldrums. Champagne no longer flowed. Men were out of work. Shops were deserted.

Bunau-Varilla pondered long and seriously on how he could exploit this situation. He was fully aware that one

thing in his favor was the 1846 treaty which permitted the
United States to send troops to maintain order along the
railroad.

Quite independently of Bunau-Varilla, a *junta,* or revolutionary committee, was very active in Panama. It was headed
by Dr. Amador Guerrero, a physician and a man who was
trusted and respected by everyone. For months in the sum-
mer of 1903 this *junta* had been secretly buying arms in the
United States and smuggling them into Panama. When the
Panamanian agents were finished, 4,000 rifles and 1,500,000
rounds of ammunition were stashed away in old warehouses
and jungle clearings. This was enough firepower to defeat
any army south of our border.

In spite of this armament, the conspirators still faced grave
problems. Word of the unrest was getting around, and rein-
forcements of Colombian troops for the garrisons in Panama
City and Colon were expected at any moment. Worst of all,
Colombia had available wicked little gunboats on each side
of the Isthmus. All the rifles in the world would be helpless
against their cannon.

In this dilemma, Dr. Amador took ship for New York. He
felt that there, somehow, all the muddled pieces of this
jigsaw could be put together. He was right.

"Accidentally" he fell in with Bunau-Varilla, who had not
yet been able to work his way out of his own blind alley. He
and Dr. Amador were made for each other.

In room 1162 of the Waldorf-Astoria, the egg of revolution was hatched. Bunau-Varilla saw the answer to all his
problems, and took over, very possibly to the relief of the
anxious emissary from Panama. He was everywhere at once.
The time for action had arrived. He talked with congress-

men, bankers, lawyers, businessmen, assistants in our State Department—even with the President of the United States!

When all was ready, Bunau-Varilla called in Dr. Amador and presented him with a "special package deal," saying in effect, "The United States can subsidize no revolution. Her honor forbids such a thing. However, when we have acted they will be in a position to offer protection."

"And what about those Colombian garrisons?" asked Dr. Amador.

Bunau-Varilla reached in his desk, pulled out a fat bag of gold coins. "Here," he said, "is one hundred thousand dollars. Pay the back salaries of the troops. Very likely this generosity will make them forget their oath to the Colombian government."

One more major point remained—the Colombian gunboats. "It will take millions to buy naval vessels capable of overwhelming these," objected Dr. Amador.

"Precisely," said Bunau-Varilla briskly. "There is no need to go to such lengths." He hesitated. "Leave this point to me. Remember that the United States is committed to maintaining order along the line of the Panama Railroad. They . . . have quite a fleet available."

The perfect revolution was thus planned, even down to a flag for the new republic, designed and hemmed by Madame Bunau-Varilla.

In return for all this, Bunau-Varilla demanded only one small thing for himself. As soon as independence was proclaimed, he wished to receive a telegraphed appointment naming him the Panamanian minister to the United States. Most reasonable.

Back in Panama, Dr. Amador unfolded the plan to his

fellow conspirators, who received it in stony silence. They heartily resented the interference of Bunau-Varilla. However, the alternatives were bleak. They had no choice. On one point, however, they remained firm. They threw out Madame Bunau-Varilla's flag and designed one of their own!

All was ready. Guns and ammunition were rushed to strategic spots. On a trumped-up invasion charge, part of the Colombian garrison was rushed off to defend the Panamanian border with Costa Rica.

A fleet of Colombian gunboats en route to pick up troops to suppress the revolution put into the coaling docks in Panama Bay. "I'm very sorry," said the Yankee foreman in charge of the bunkers. "We are all out of coal. Barely enough to keep the trains running. Come back next week." The gunboats retired to anchor in the harbor with scarcely enough fuel to keep up a head of steam.

In Colon, the *Nashville*, an American cruiser happened to come into port. Everything was quiet. Commander Hubbard saw no disturbance that would serve as justification for landing his marines and bluejackets.

During the night a large Colombian warship, the *Cartagena*, warped up to the dock and began debarking about five hundred soldiers, along with equipment, women and children.

In response to Hubbard's questions, General Tovar smoothly explained that this was just part of a routine transfer of garrison troops. There was no rioting, no shooting. All was quiet.

The Colombian troops made ready to ride across the Isthmus to Panama City. The Panama Railroad was treaty-bound to transport government troops, and the manager knew that soon General Tovar would be demanding passage. Accordingly, he quickly shunted all his rolling stock out of town, *except* one locomotive and a parlor car which he kept in the Colon station.

Soon General Tovar and his staff were comfortably seated in the parlor car, on their way across. "The rest of the troops," the manager courteously explained, "will make the crossing the moment cars are available."

The officers arrived in Panama City, and after a grand reception were taken prisoner by the revolutionists. The hero of the *coup* was a diminutive general, Esteban Huertas, commander of the Colombian garrison. Now that the revolutionaries had paid his salary up to date, he was only too glad to put his former bosses in jail.

Independence was a fact on the Pacific side. The city exploded in jubilation, the continual popping of Winchesters adding to the excitement. The gunboats in the bay lobbed two shells over the town. One hit a donkey and the other killed a Chinese shopkeeper, the only casualty of the revolt.

On the Atlantic side, matters were not so simple. Colonel Torres, the officer commanding the troops camped with their families in the streets of Colon, demanded transportation for himself and his soldiers to Panama City. The railroad yards were by now full of rolling stock. The manager was most cordial. The fare, he said, "comes to over two thousand dollars for all these troops." He was gambling on the probability that Torres had not read the treaty which stated that soldiers were to be transported free of charge. Torres had no idea of the treaty, and of course, he had no such sum of money. He and his men stayed right there.

Now word leaked out about events in Panama City.

Colonel Torres immediately announced to the American consul that he would kill every American in town unless General Tovar and the other officers were released. He marched on the railroad determined to take it by force.

Now Commander Hubbard could act. Here was riot, violence. He deployed his marines back of cotton bales in the stone railroad station and ordered all American civilians to take refuge on two ocean liners conveniently tied up at the docks.

As battle was about to begin, another American ship, the *Dixie*, slipped into port and started unloading more marines. Word got out that other United States naval vessels, also just by chance, were heading under forced draft for the Isthmus!

Colonel Torres was a thoughtful man. Perhaps he had been too rash. When his temper cooled, he called off his men, and the marines returned to their ships. The war was over. Panama was a free republic.

At 3:00 P.M. on November 4, 1903, a mammoth independence celebration was held in Cathedral Plaza. General Esteban Huertas was the hero of the moment. He was carried by his joyful soldiers in a chair draped with royal purple. On his right strode the American consul, carrying the Stars and Stripes; to his left walked Dr. Amador, bearing the brand-new flag of the republic. It was a real, satisfying fiesta.

Two days later, on November 6, President Theodore Roosevelt extended official recognition to the new nation— before many citizens even knew what had happened and certainly before anyone in Colombia had a true picture of the situation. It was a full twenty-one years later that Colombia received an apology from our government and a $25 million appeasement offering.

And what of the man behind all this—the French Machia-velli, Bunau-Varilla? Anxiously he haunted the cable office in New York. Finally the cable arrived—he was appointed "Envoy Extraordinary and Minister Plenipotentiary to the Government of the United States with full power for politi-cal and financial negotiations."

Shortly afterward Dr. Amador and a delegation arrived in Washington to discuss a Canal treaty with the United States, but they were too late. Bunau-Varilla had put the finishing touches to his master plan. The treaty, signed, sealed and approved, was delivered to an astounded Dr. Amador!

Panama got $10 million for the Canal concession, plus a yearly annuity of $250,000. The rights granted to the United States in Bunau-Varilla's treaty were possibly as good as those Dr. Amador or anyone else could have gotten.

Certainly it was to Panama's advantage to have a powerful friend who would not only construct the Canal, but also guarantee her independence against all comers. The abrupt manner in which it was done, however, and the acceptance by the United States of the highhanded actions of Bunau-Varilla, who was a French citizen, rankled deeply. Perhaps Dr. Amador's philosophic statement at the time sums up the general feeling: "At any rate," he said, "Panama will get rid of the yellow fever." The precipitate actions of the United States only a few days before the revolution had likewise alienated Colombia.

These acts paved the way for immediate work on the Canal. President Roosevelt commented later on that it was better to have done what they did to get the Canal built and debate *him* for fifty years, than to have done nothing at all, letting the whole project languish.

One other item needs explaining, but there seems to be little explanation. What happened to the $40 million paid to the French Canal interests? Presumably the money was paid to the investment firm of J. P. Morgan & Co. for disbursement to the clamoring French stockholders.

Sullivan and Cromwell, the law firm which represented the French, presented a bill for $800,000 including $60,000 for an American political party. How that got in there we'll never know. Bunau-Varilla and his associates received a cut estimated by people who hated him at a modest $16 million. The balance went to bondholders at 11 per cent of the face value of their bonds. There were those who said the bondholders were speculators who bought up at a very low price all the bonds they could lay their hands on, and so there was nothing left over for ordinary French shareholders.

Documents, data, testimony, piled up in various investigations, but somehow they further confused an already obscure transaction. Today, as then, nobody *really* knows who got that $40 million.

Chapter 8

The United States was now the undisputed landlord of one of the most valuable pieces of real estate on earth. In their own eyes, and in those of the world, they were committed to bring to reality one of man's oldest dreams—to build across this piece of land a canal from the Pacific to the Atlantic.

Almost before the ink was dry on the treaty with the brand-new Republic of Panama, President Roosevelt called America to action as though to sacred patriotic duty. A full month before Second Lieutenant Mark Brooke watched the tricolor come fluttering down from the French Canal Company headquarters, and the Stars and Stripes rise to take its place, an eminent commission was on its way to the Isthmus. These engineers from every corner of the nation had been hastily summoned to Washington on four days notice. Burning with enthusiasm, they prepared to leave for Panama with instructions to get the dirt flying.

If the Isthmus of Panama was one of the world's most valuable pieces of real estate, it was at the same time from almost any point of view one of the most depressing and formidable. Rain, measured in feet, not inches, fell for about ten months out of the year, turning the land into a quaking

93

mire. The run-off over the centuries had drained clay and silt into the seas so that the coastlines at low tide were nothing more than miles of stinking, exposed mudflat. The jungle was terrifying with its strange animals and birds, its deadly snakes, its shrieking jaguars. In it lurked red ants which could sting a man's body to flaming fire and insects which burrowed in his skin to lay their eggs.

This land was crisscrossed with undependable rivers, and down its middle ran the cordillera, or hump. This backbone was devilishly hard to dig and blast loose but once disturbed could not be controlled.

During the dry season, when the sun blazed fiercely and trade winds blew without stopping, the jungle and the savannas seared and turned yellow, the thirst a palpable and brooding thing. The mud and silt baked hard, then easily pulverized to irritating and nauseous dust.

Before the distinguished group of engineers left the United States for the Isthmus, it was joined by an additional man. He wasn't even a member of the august body, but was more like a hired hand, with no voice in what was or was not to be done. His name was Major William Crawford Gorgas; he was an unassuming and likable army medico. Gorgas had made a name for himself assisting in the sanitation work in Havana during and after the Spanish-American War. He was regarded as one of the foremost American authorities on tropical diseases.

That a medical man was even included at all in this first, "hurry-up" appraisal of America's new property was a wonder. Almost as an afterthought, it seems, somebody remembered that hideous diseases made the Isthmus a place of death, and that something probably had better be done about it.

Since white men first put in an appearance, the whole range of tropical and subtropical maladies had at one time or another swept the Isthmus, sometimes mildly and at other times with epidemic violence. Smallpox, Asiatic cholera, typhoid, beriberi, an awesome list of deadly dysenteries, leprosy, had all visited Panama.

The most familiar and lethal killers of all, of course, were malaria and yellow fever—the latter dubbed "yellow jack" by generations of seafaring men. The terrible part played by mosquitoes in the spread of these diseases had been first advanced as a theory by Dr. Donald Ross, a Scotch physician in the Indian civil service. His work was advanced and practical application given it by American army surgeons struggling to eliminate the pestilences from Havana. Gorgas was included in these Army sanitation teams and worked with such men as Majors Walter Reed, Jesse Lazear, and Carroll. Major Lazear sacrificed his life to test the theories when he bravely allowed himself to be bitten by a mosquito believed to be carrying yellow jack.

Major Gorgas must have shuddered when he first saw the Isthmus. Conditions were perfect for the spread of disease. Water was everywhere—in swamps, puddles, stagnant pools, rain buckets, barrels. The streets of the squalid towns were ankle deep in mud when wet and boiling with germ-laden dust when dry. Drinking water was carried about by vendors in large barrels and jars. There were no sewage nor garbage facilities. The inhabitants blithely tossed the slops into the streets. Markets were filthy, rat-infested sheds in which meat and other foods were hung in the open, exposed to dirt and to millions of buzzing flies. At night, the whining of mosquitoes was more familiar than the chirp of cicadas.

Laborers lived in miserable huts, many of which were built on piers or stilts over the mud. The "quality" had more elegant homes, but they too drank dirty water, scratched fleas, slapped mosquitoes and waded in the mud. Disease played no favorites—over mansions and shanties alike hung the same dark shadows of sudden and inexplicable death.

Of all those Americans who arrived on that first visit to Panama in March of 1904, only Major Gorgas had any idea of the gigantic sanitation job which lay ahead if the Canal were ever going to be built. His voice was a small and unimportant one, however. It was lost in the excitement and the driving urge to get on with the job, to get the Canal started.

Like new tenants anywhere, the Isthmian Canal Commission poked into every nook and corner to see what the previous occupants had left behind. They found plenty, and they were appalled by their discoveries!

The Isthmus was like a deserted battlefield, littered from one end to the other with the debris of a retreating, defeated army. Whole villages slowly surrendered to the jungle. Mile upon mile of rolling equipment, sadly sinking into the mud, was fit only for the junk heaps. The commission members gaped at enormous roundhouses whose walls and roofs were held up by the rusting locomotives inside. In rickety warehouses and piled outside under the sky were car wheels, giant hammers, lathes, forges, boilers, milling machines—all the panoply of modern industrial might—piled helter-skelter, forgotten, ruined, abandoned in melancholy profusion.

However, on the credit side, there was a great deal of

usable equipment and gradually it came to light. Enormous amounts of machinery could be salvaged. Nearly fifteen hundred French buildings of various sizes could be hacked free of the jungle and made habitable. Thousands of careful and very accurate surveys and topographical maps were well preserved. About half of the sixty million cubic yards of earth which the French had excavated were extremely valuable. The continental divide had been lowered 160 feet. Fairly good ports and docks existed on each side of the Isthmus, and from them serviceable deep-water channels were dredged inland.

On top of all this, there was something else left to the United States upon which no value could be placed. It was worth more perhaps than all the material items put together. This was knowledge. The French had learned some terrible lessons—among them what kind of machinery worked, and what didn't. They had demonstrated that while a sea-level canal might be better in the long run, it would be incredibly difficult to build. They had proved in the most agonizing way possible that if something were not done to make the Isthmus a more healthful place, very possibly *nobody* would ever build the Canal.

In spite of first impressions, in spite of cynicism about the French effort, Uncle Sam got his money's worth.

Sticking to the mandate to make the dirt fly, the commission reasoned that the first thing was to get men working. Up in the cuts about seven hundred laborers, the remnants of once enormous French forces, scratched away at the earth, assisted by three clattering little shovels and a fleet of diminutive Belgian flatcars and locomotives. It was concluded that thousands of men could be put to work here.

The commission returned to Washington and immediately the word for recruits went out. Men flocked to the colors and soon were streaming southward.

Among them were four surveying teams which were to explore the Isthmus thoroughly and pick out a likely route for the future Canal. These teams were the famed "Tropic Tramps"—the spearhead of all our effort. John F. Wallace, an extremely competent engineer and general manager of the Illinois Central Railroad, was top man.

In time the "Tropic Tramps" emerged from the jungles with their reports. The route which they recommended followed almost exactly that which Pascual de Andagoya had selected for the king of Spain in 1534!

At the moment John Wallace was not particularly interested in routes for the Canal! He had other, more immediate problems and they backed all the way from Panama to Washington.

From the very beginning, he faced a two-headed dragon. On one side America screamed loudly for action. Get that Canal rolling! Immediately! On the other side, the commission in Washington buried him in red tape and in decisions which had nothing to do with actual conditions in Panama.

Everything from a nursing bottle for use in a hospital to a railroad locomotive had to be approved, signed and countersigned in Washington. The commissioners kept in mind Andagoya's remark that to build the Canal "would exhaust the richest treasury in all of Christendom." They also had very much before them the French record of mismanagement. To a man they were determined that no such thing would happen to the American effort. "Whether the Canal is ever opened or not, there will be no charges of graft or waste brought against this body" was the answer to desperate requests for supplies. They stuck to this policy. They and they alone would decide what was needed on the Isthmus, and never mind what the engineers said.

To the commissioners most of the urgent appeals from Panama seemed to have little to do with constructing a Canal. Why did sewers in Panama City, miles from the Canal Zone, have to be built immediately? Why were expensive, modern cranes on the docks so necessary right now? And in the name of heaven, why was it so important to feed West Indian laborers their accustomed diet of rice and salted Newfoundland codfish in order to get a good day's work out of them?

Thus Wallace was forced to "dig" before he was ready to do so. And he was hamstrung by a commission back in the States which either prevented him outright from doing what needed to be done, or slowed down top priority requests to the point where everything had to be done backwards.

One of Wallace's first tasks, before he could even try to comply with the frantic requests to get the dirt flying, was to unscramble the havoc left by the French. Locomotives must be overhauled, dredges repaired, flatcars put into serviceable condition and railroad spurs built. All this required men, and they swelled an already overburdened and staggering organization. Men must be fed and they must be housed, and for this, buildings are required and so lumber is needed.

Even though great stands of fine hardwood trees grew on the Isthmus, transportation difficulties were so great that all wood had to come from the States. The commission finally approved vast lumber shipments from the Pacific Northwest. But proper railroad sidings and dock facilities had not yet been constructed when the lumber ships began arriving. Panama Bay was clogged with them. Finally, their cargoes were heaved overboard, made into rafts, floated ashore and then carried across mud flats stick by stick, by long lines of laborers, and dumped in awesome and confusing piles. It took months to straighten out the resultant mess.

Not only must men be fed and housed, but on the Isthmus, their health must also be most carefully guarded. A sanitation program was inaugurated, and Dr. Gorgas, now promoted to colonel, was placed in charge.

By 1904 there should not have been any argument or question on this point, but ignorance and the timorous, pinchpenny attitudes back in Washington very nearly caused the collapse of the entire effort. Almost immediately, Gorgas found that his recommendations and requisitions were either ignored, trimmed or most reluctantly filled. The commission simply could not understand all the hullaballoo about health conditions. The feeling seemed to be that the United States had gone to Panama to build a canal, not to turn it into a spotless tropical resort.

Finally convinced that sewage facilities and clean drinking water were necessary in Panama City for the general health of the entire Isthmus, the commission gave grudging approval. Ditches were dug, but then the shipments of expensive pipe were held up. The city was crisscrossed by slimy, foul, water-filled trenches which added to the stink and the general confusion.

Only half of Gorgas' urgent request for copper screening, to be put on the windows of living quarters, was approved. After all, screens were quite a luxury. He was told that workmen back in the States didn't seem to need screens on

their homes! Gorgas was advised to screen half the windows
and board the rest up solid.

He was balked or slowed in every direction. When he
asked for expensive fumigants, only a fraction of his requests was filled. No one could see why tumble-down Negro
shacks had to be fumigated and cleaned. Probably better to
burn them down in the first place! Eyebrows were lifted
when he insisted that whole native villages which were infected with malaria or yellow jack had to be moved bodily
to new locations outside the Canal Zone. It seemed a sheer
waste of money when Gorgas organized teams to trim and
cut grass and shrubs along the edges of streams or near
dwellings. The laughter echoed from Panama to Washington
when this "crackpot" medico stated that every last swamp
and puddle on the Canal Zone had to be drained! Americans
had come to the Isthmus to build a Big Ditch, not a maze of
tiny ones!

Colonel Gorgas' whole concern, his obsession about mosquitoes, was highly suspect by many people—Panamanians
and Americans. From time immemorial, Isthmian fevers were
"known" to have been caused by the white mists which rose
like evil ghosts out of the ocean, the mud flats, the disturbed earth. The newfangled notion that malaria and yellow jack were caused by the bite of a mosquito was an innovation—and something of a joke.

From the very beginning the whole sanitation effort was
regarded as a debatable luxury and was ridiculed. The
danger was whitewashed, even by people on the Isthmus
who should have known better. The American minister to
Panama, in a magazine article, lauded the sanitation work to
the skies and then went on to say that "at this time there is

no more danger from yellow fever in Panama than there is from grippe and pneumonia in the States." Even as late as June, in 1905, one of the local newspapers, the *Diario de Panama,* commenting on the entire plan for the Canal, wrote ". . . it is an error as great as that of fumigating all the houses in Panama to destroy mosquitoes or try to stamp out yellow fever on the Isthmus. To attempt it is a dream, an illusion, perhaps simply a case of American boasting."

In spite of the derision and the criticism, Colonel Gorgas quietly and doggedly kept to his task, doing what he could. He knew that if the American attempt to build the Canal were not to meet the same end as the French effort, the houses would have to be screened, the swamps drained, the grass cut, the huts fumigated, the mosquitoes killed. He knew that sooner or later his time would come and that all the "foolish" and expensive measures he insisted upon would have to be done. Meanwhile, he kept his fingers crossed.

The wheels of the entire Canal project ground slower and slower, choked and plugged by overcautiousness and by red tape. From home came insistent cries for action for the dirt to fly. From the Isthmus came cries for a little sanity, for a little common sense—appeals to let competent people on the job decide what should be done first and how to do it. Urgent cables clicked northward over the wires in a steady stream until the commission decided that their use was to be discontinued. They were too expensive! Henceforward, letters were to be written.

During this first year, when he could find time from pressing local matters, Wallace made several trips to Washington to plead for a little order. The trips were in vain. Finally, in near desperation, he appealed directly to President Roosevelt. The President was also more than fed up by now, and he moved with great speed. He agreed 100 per cent with Wallace in all that was asked. In spite of great opposition, Roosevelt appointed a new commission and greatly increased Wallace's power to deal with problems as they arose on the scene of action.

The chief engineer returned to the Isthmus, but as far as he was concerned, the change in policy had come too late. A week after his arrival back on the job, he cabled his resignation. Some say he received offers elsewhere for a better position. Others say he had developed a morbid fear of the fevers. Most agree, however, that Wallace was a broken man, that he had collapsed under the accumulated burden of a whole year's terrible frustration and strain.

During the last weeks of Wallace's reign, the catastrophe which Colonel Gorgas had so long feared took place. It might very well have put a quick end to all hopes for the Canal. As though tired of these dilatory humans, and all their procrastination, Panama showed her teeth. A violent yellow fever epidemic broke out. If Wallace and Gorgas had been heeded, it might never have happened.

The Isthmus reeled under the impact—there were 250 cases in two months. Due to the work which Gorgas and his crews had managed to complete, the mortality was mercifully low, but it destroyed the morale and the spirit of the workers who had come to Panama. The word got around at home that all was not well at the site of the Canal, and letters from wives and sweethearts streamed from the United States, begging the men to return . . . before they ended up like all those Frenchmen! Steamship offices were swamped by requests for passage out of Panama.

During this first year, much honest work had been done, but the project was a shambles. If Wallace had been left to his own devices and had been permitted to spend time and money as he wished on sanitation and organization, the blunders of this terrible year might have been avoided.

Chapter 9

John F. Stevens stood on a flatcar on a Panama Railroad siding at a work camp. He looked down on the listless and dispirited group of men who had come to meet him.

He was a tall, broad-shouldered, powerful man, extremely handsome with dark, wavy hair and light eyes. He sported a big, jet-black moustache. He took the butt of a huge cigar from his mouth, threw it away, then lit another one. Between puffs, staring at the crowd, he said, "There's nothing wrong with you men except yellow fever, malaria . . ." Between the rolling clouds of smoke, Stevens inspected the cigar critically, the way a man does who loves his smokes. Then he continued. ". . . yellow fever, malaria . . . and cold feet. Of the three, the last is the most serious."

There was a little uncomfortable grinning and considerable muttering among the men. "Cold feet?" shouted a voice. "Didn't you see that pile of coffins on the dock?"

"Yes, I saw 'em," Stevens grunted, "but if you worried less and worked more you'd be better off."

More puffing. More muttering among the men. Then Stevens said, "There's nobody working around here except the ants and the typists. And that's going to change."

The tension vanished like magic. The men looked at their

new chief engineer, clad in an old slouch hat and overalls, and laughed.

This was Stevens' second day on the job and his first tour along the route. Similar scenes took place from one end of the line to the other. Here was a man the "roughnecks," as the old-time ditchdiggers were called, could understand. He was rough, tough, driving, hard, with no trace of elegance in his manner. He knew what he was doing and he had learned his trade the hard way—not in universities, but in the West, building railroads.

The Panama Canal didn't awe John Stevens. Bridges, tunnels, excavations, the management of rowdy labor camps, were nothing new to him.

Such a man needed a nickname and it was quickly found. "Big Smoke Stevens" he was called and the name stuck. Gleefully, the roughnecks found out that among the Indians of the Northwest, he was called "Chief Big Smoke"!

On this first trip, Big Smoke found that the men in the camps were actually hungry, so poor was the distribution system of food. His first official act was to send out loaded commissary trains all along the line. It worked like magic. Within two days the exodus of men from the Isthmus had ceased. Confidence in themselves and in their chief engineer returned. Morale and spirits soared.

President Roosevelt appointed a new commission with orders that at least three of the members were to be on the Isthmus at all times to see for themselves what was going on. If this didn't work, Stevens was to go directly over their heads and report to the White House.

The big job picked up speed. Shortly not only ants and typists were busy. The roughnecks pitched in with a will—

but they weren't working on the Canal! Big Smoke was a first-things-first man. He calmly suspended all digging while the entire mess was straightened out. "Digging," he said, "is the least of all."

The manager of the railroad proudly cited the road's perfect safety record. "There hasn't been a collision in a year."

Stevens puffed violently and stared down into the vast ravine of the cut. He looked at the idle steam shovels, saw the men lounging about. He glared at the empty flatcars that couldn't be loaded because full cars blocked the tracks.

"At least," he said, "a collision has some good points. It shows that trains are moving."

The men within earshot howled. Rapidly the word spread. This new chief engineer was quite a man.

For five days not a shovelful of earth was moved in the cut. All hands pitched in to build new sidings, clear away debris, lay new tracks, reroute the full spoil trains and get the empties back quickly.

The railroad had first priority not only in the cuts, but across the entire Isthmus. Nothing could be done until the problem of transportation was licked. Things had to be gotten out from under foot and taken where they were needed. Room had to be made for the additional supplies that were constantly unloaded from the ships.

Besides the railroad, other things were higher on Stevens' priority list than digging a Canal. Nearly a full year was to pass before excavating crews were back up to strength.

Men were assigned to those tasks which had to be completed *first*. Quarters were built, good commissaries established, kitchens and mess halls organized, dispensaries and hospitals put into operation. The beginnings of an efficient fire department, courts, a police system and waterworks were undertaken. In short, all those things which were imperative if the Canal were ever to be built at all were attended to.

The cries to "make the dirt fly" continued at home. Chairman Theodore P. Shonts of the Canal commission, President Roosevelt and Stevens ignored them. The dirt would fly soon enough, they hoped, but right now first things had to come first. At last tough, hard men, the only kind that could succeed in such a situation, were in charge.

Perhaps of all the men on the job, none had suffered a greater share of abuse than Colonel Gorgas. Of the programs undertaken on the Isthmus, that of sanitation had been most blocked and criticized. Now, under the common-sense policy of Stevens' regime, all this was changed. Panama *must* be cleaned up! The phrase became a battle slogan. Included in the new sanitation program was not only the Canal Zone, but the adjacent areas of the republic as well. Gorgas was given everything he wanted for an all-out assault on filth and on disease—particularly on malaria and yellow fever.

All buildings were screened and crews of men made regular rounds, searching like detectives, inspecting for the tiniest hole or puncture. The whine of a mosquito in a home was the signal for the head of the family to get on the telephone and call the sanitation office. Crews of men converged on the offending building like firemen responding to a four-alarm blaze. They searched until the luckless bug was found, chloroformed and taken to the laboratory for examination. If it was a malaria or yellow fever mosquito, and anyone had been bitten, that unfortunate person was immediately quarantined and started on massive doses of "Panama cocktails" —quinine.

Swamps and puddles and stagnant pools were drained. Laborers and highly paid engineers alike, who had been digging the Big Ditch in the mountains, now found themselves digging networks of small drainage ditches that spread everywhere like a spiderweb. Paris green—a powerful insecticide—was dripped day and night from barrels into slow-moving streams. A thin film of oil, which prevented mosquito wrigglers from breathing, was spread over all standing water which could not be drained off. Grass and shrubbery were trimmed, and those dark, moist, shady spots favored for breeding by yellow fever mosquitoes were cleaned out.

Mop-up battalions in Colon and Panama City were increased. Houses—all of them, from the greatest to the smallest—were evacuated. Cracks were sealed with paper and paste and the buildings fumigated. After the dead mosquitoes and other assorted bugs were swept out, the dwellings were returned to their owners, probably cleaner than they had been in a long time. Cooking utensils, rain barrels, flower pots, empty cans—anything that could harbor a stagnant bit of water—were destroyed. Even in the churches baptismal fonts were suspect, and where necessary, the holy water and any wriggling mosquito larvae were removed. Sewage systems were installed. Garbage collectors began making regular rounds. Years of accumulated filth in the public markets was removed. Squads of men whose sole business was to trap rats moved back and forth from one end of the cities to the other. The long-delayed water pipes were laid and on the fourth of July, the water was turned on. "Fresh Water Day" brought out a mighty celebration!

Everything that money, hard work, medical knowledge and human ingenuity could do was done to make the Isthmus a safe, healthful place in which to live. Eventually, the Isthmus was transformed from one of the world's worst pestholes into a place fit for human habitation. Had this not been done, the Panama Canal might never have been built. If credit for the successful completion of the Canal could be assigned to any one man, Colonel William C. Gorgas' name would rate high on the list. Without his skill, his knowledge and his vision, the vast engineering and industrial might brought to bear on the job would have amounted to nothing.

Meanwhile, from one end of the gigantic project to the other, night and day, Chief Engineer John Stevens struggled to bring order out of chaos. Puffing his big black stogies, clad always in slouch hat and overalls, he was everywhere. He missed nothing. With his quick banter and his salty humor he asked for and received heroic efforts from his men.

Stevens spurned the fancy quarters set aside for the chief engineer and moved into a screened, tin-roof shack out above the cuts. He rode locomotives, flatcars, and work trains instead of the plush parlor car. When hungry, he bobbed up in the messes in the field and ate with the crews. On each table, along with the salt, pepper, and sugar, were canisters of quinine, and Stevens grumbled just as much as any of his men as he downed the prescribed dose of the bitter and much-hated drug.

His work days were twelve, fifteen and eighteen hours. Once he told an associate that "I know it is weak to complain of being tired, but the fact is I've only had five hours of sleep in the last sixty."

Such vitality and drive could have but one result: very

shortly, the dirt did begin to fly. By the end of a year, more than two thousand men were at work in the cuts. Gigantic steam shovels bit their way into the cordillera. New locomotives hauled away the spoil on flatcars which rolled on renovated and strategically located track systems. The spoil was unloaded at new dumps which gradually built up and hardened and became useful building sites.

Men began to write home and urge friends and relatives to come to the Isthmus. A man could live here now. The big job was beginning to roll, and it was something in which to take pride.

In addition to skilled American personnel, thousands upon thousands of laborers were needed. During Stevens' regime, the vanguard started rolling in. West Indians, Greeks, Frenchmen came from all over the world as the word went out that there were jobs begging in Panama. Stevens especially favored the Spaniards. These tough, hard-working men from the plains and high mountains of Spain were people he liked and understood. He set up an office in Paris for their recruitment, and eventually over seven thousand of these industrious and frugal workers were hired and brought to the Isthmus.

One terribly vexing problem remained to be solved. Daily it became more acute and clamored for a solution. The type of canal which was to built had not yet been determined. Was it to be a sea-level waterway, or was it to be a high-level lock canal?

As time went on, Stevens' anxiety increased. There was a vast amount of work which could be done that would be useful for *either* type. The operating organization—towns, hospitals, commissaries, sanitation and so on—would be the same in either case. A certain amount of dredging, a certain amount of work in the cuts could be accomplished. There was a point, however, beyond which it would be impossible to go unless the decision were made. Work was going so fast that Stevens and his men were rapidly reaching this crucial point. If a lock canal were built, the railroad must be rerouted as the bed would be covered by the lake, which would spread across much of the interior. The same with many towns already existing, or contemplated. Spoil was piling up. Where was it to be dumped? Put here it would interfere with a lock canal but not a sea-level canal. Put another place, the opposite condition would be true.

Stevens had very early begun to agitate for a decision, but none was forthcoming for a long, long time. At first he had been in favor of a sea-level canal, but as he looked over the giant, ever-deepening cuts, his skilled engineer's eyes began to see signs of the terrible problems of slides that were sure to come, which would be magnified if they had to dig down to sea level. He doubted Congress would ever appropriate enough money for such a long and costly job.

He talked with marine experts and began to see some of the hazards to ships which such a canal would be. The narrow, tortuous waterway would be turbulent with eddies and currents caused by tides and rivers pouring into it. Steering would be very difficult for ships. It would be extremely dangerous for a big vessel because even going very slowly, the slightest contact with the rock walls could tear out her plates and sink her, blocking the channel.

Roosevelt had long since appointed a planning board to grapple with this vital problem. It struggled through interminable meetings and consultations. At long last, in January of 1906 it submitted to the President a recommendation for a sea-level canal. Roosevelt sided with Stevens in favoring a lock canal, and so he simply passed the report on to the Senate with his comments.

Time dragged on. Stevens was running out of work on the Isthmus; the likelihood arose that he would have to start discharging men. Finally, on May 17 the Committee on Interoceanic Canals of the Senate made its report. They had decided in favor of a sea-level waterway.

Stevens was stunned but the battle was not yet over. The showdown would come on the floor of the Senate. He was hastily summoned to Washington and immediately plunged into the thick of the fight. He wrote letters and memos; he made speeches, buttonholed congressmen. He argued with Secretary of War William Howard Taft and kept up Roosevelt's courage when the President seemed to waver. At last the question came to a vote on June 21, 1906. *Three years* after the revolution in Panama and the purchase of rights to build the Canal, a decision was made. By a weak majority, the Senate voted for a lock canal.

Stevens returned to the Isthmus on the Fourth of July. During his two-month absence everything had run smoothly. Machinery and equipment were pouring in on ships. More men were arriving and getting settled. Everything was poised for the big push. Now that the decision as to canal type had been made, the real work was ready to start.

Stevens felt that the opening of the Canal would depend upon the completion of the locks and dam at Gatun on the Atlantic side. The amount of work and construction which must be crammed into this small area was stupendous. He looked over the tranquil site and made a guess. "The Canal will be opened for traffic on January 1, 1915. Now get to work."

The men jumped. They started to hack out the jungle, survey for the dam, take soundings for bedrock, plan for the relocation of the railroad and numerous towns when the lake rose.

One more big problem remained. *Who* was going to build the Canal? The government or private contractors?

Chairman Theodore P. Shonts, a rugged individualist and a railroad builder himself, favored the contractors. Stevens favored the government. He had worked hard building an organization capable of doing the job, and he reacted instinctively against turning it over to private people whose main purpose must be to make a profit.

At the moment Shonts was in Washington and Stevens was far off in Panama. Shonts persuaded Roosevelt on the contractor idea and bids were let. Stevens objected in no uncertain terms. When the bids came in they were all rejected on grounds that they did not conform to specifications. The real reason was very likely that in his heart President Roosevelt agreed with Stevens. The work was a public project and should be done by the government. He felt that the people agreed with this.

Chairman Shonts resigned and in a swift move to consolidate authority, Roosevelt combined the offices of chairman of the commission and chief engineer in one. Stevens was appointed.

Thus the situation was precisely as Stevens wished it to be. As engineer on duty in Panama, he had unlimited authority and power, and back of him was a President who believed in him fully.

On the Isthmus, the roughnecks went wild. Big Smoke was in the saddle. The steam shovels were on the way. Nothing could stop them now.

In November of 1906 Roosevelt paid a visit to the scene —the first time a President had ever been outside continental United States during a term of office. He came during the rainy season because he wanted to see the Isthmus under the most trying conditions. And he did. Day after day rain poured from a leaden sky. The streets were awash. Garbage flowed in rivers down those gutters which had been completed. However, it was a triumphant and joyous tour. Never losing his grin, Roosevelt strode from one end of the Canal Zone to the other.

When he arrived back in the States his report to the nation was enthusiastic. His praise of Stevens was almost eloquent. Stevens was the man of the hour. He would get that Canal built if anyone could.

And then, on April 1, 1907, Stevens resigned.

There are many stories. One of them goes like this: An intimate friend of Stevens' came into his office and Stevens showed him a letter he had just written.

"Read this," said Big Smoke. "I've just been easing my mind to T. R. It's a hot one, isn't it?"

"But," said the friend, "this is the same as a letter of resignation."

Stevens laughed. "Why, I've said that kind of thing to the colonel a dozen times. He knows I don't mean to quit this job."

Three hours after the letter reached Washington, Stevens received a cablegram. It read: "Your resignation accepted."

Other stories say that Big Smoke was fed up having to play

politician and having to submit to endless government red tape. He detested the paper work and there were reams of it daily. He was not a socializer and had his fill entertaining the constant stream of "important visitors" and congressmen, and really wanted out. He felt his job was done. He had promised Roosevelt when he took over that he would get the project on its feet and not leave until everything was set to go. In a sense, the job was over. From now on it was mainly a matter of pouring concrete and digging dirt.

Whatever the *real* reason, it remained a secret. Yet to be named was his successor.

Chapter 10

On a spring evening in Washington, in 1907, George Washington Goethals, a major in the Corps of Engineers of the United States Army, was entertaining a brother officer at dinner in his home. A messenger arrived from the White House requesting Goethals to present himself at the offices of the President at 9:30 the following morning.

Goethals was a fine officer of the old school. He was a West Pointer, with a good but not spectacular record behind him. His specialty was locks and dams. He was not accustomed to hobnobbing with the Big Brass, and he was puzzled by the summons.

He called the President's office to confirm the appointment and a moment later returned to his wife and guest even more bewildered. "The President wants to see me right away," he announced. In a short while he was on his way to the White House. By 10:30 that evening his suspense was over.

President Roosevelt told him in effect that he was sick and tired of so many changes in Panama. He had tried two civilians and they had quit on him. He was turning the job over to the army, to men who were under orders and could not resign. Goethals had been selected for the job of chief engineer.

In one sweeping Rooseveltian gesture, all interference from commissions and politicians was abolished. The new appointee had complete, nearly dictatorial powers to do whatever might be necessary to get the job going and see it through to a finish.

The news of Stevens' resignation and the appointment of an army officer fell with a sodden plop on the nation and particularly on those Americans working in Panama. Their idolized Big Smoke, with his rough talk, ready understanding and quick humor, was leaving. In his place was an unknown quantity, possibly a stiff military martinet. Salutes, regimentation, even martial law very possibly would be the order of the day. The men pictured themselves marching off to work each day in formation, with picks and shovels at smart shoulder arms. Delegations were sent to Big Smoke's office, hoping to be told there was a mistake or to induce him to withdraw the resignation. The effort was hopeless.

Clawing steam shovels came to a rest; trains halted. Groups of men stood about talking dispiritedly, trying to figure out what to do. By nightfall a petition was circulating. Already it had four thousand names on it, and two days later the total was ten thousand, including practically every American working on the Canal. The petition read, "Please withdraw your resignation and remain in charge of our work. We will show our appreciation and loyalty by working for you even harder than we have up to this time."

Nothing had any effect. Stevens was leaving. With deep reservations the men awaited the arrival of the army.

In contrast to the exuberant, rousing celebrations which always welcomed important newcomers to the Isthmus, Goethals' reception was solemn and restrained. A smoker was finally arranged in his honor. It turned into a sarcastic denunciation of the army and militarism, and a eulogy for Stevens.

When everyone had had his fun, Goethals rose to speak. Less colorful than Stevens, there was nevertheless something determined and trustworthy in his quiet demeanor and in the steady gaze of his blue eyes. He wasn't in uniform, and in fact, during his entire tenure on the Isthmus, he was never seen in one. As Goethals looked at the men seated in the Corozal Clubhouse, he felt their resentment, but his words were reassuring. Among other things, he told his listeners, "I am no longer a commander in the United States Army. I consider that I am commanding the Army of Panama and that the enemy we are going to combat is the Culebra Cut and the locks and dams at both ends of the Canal, and any man here who does his duty will never have any cause to complain of militarism."

The men decided the least they could do was to give this quiet officer a break. They never regretted it.

Goethals had visited the Canal project only very briefly before, and really had very little idea of the true situation. His notions were preconceived by what he had heard and read in the States, and as usual, the newspapers were having a field day chronicling the "deplorable" state of affairs on the Isthmus.

If Goethals had any idea that he was being brought in as a "canal doctor" to try and save an ailing patient, it was very speedily dispelled as Stevens escorted him about the Isthmus. He had the grace and the honesty to say so in letters and reports:

". . . there is nothing left for us to do but just have the organization continue in the good work which it has done and is doing. I cannot see why he has resigned. . . . Mr. Stevens has done work for which he will never get any credit. . . ." And, "People talk about the success of the army engineer in Panama. . . . It is fortunate that Mr. Stevens preceded us. . . . The world cannot give him too much credit."

Just what was this "enemy" which Goethal's called upon the Army of Panama to combat? We've talked about channels and cuts and rivers and lakes. It is time now to see where and how all of these things interconnect and how they function together to form a path for great ocean-going ships.

When we think of a canal, ordinarily something like an irrigation ditch comes to mind. The canal at Suez is a perfect example. It is a ditchdigger's dream. Scooped out of the sand right down to sea level, it functions exactly like an extension of the sea—an inlet, a bay, a port, a channel—filled with salt water.

On the other hand, the Panama Canal is a fresh-water canal. It is a waterway made possible by locks and dams and a huge lake which straddles the Isthmus high above the level of the oceans. Rather than a part of the marine system, the Canal seems more like a factory. In a tropic setting, it is an enormous collection of marvelous machinery and concrete which operates as smoothly and precisely as a fine, jeweled watch.

Gatun Locks

Miraflores Locks
Miraflores Lake
Pedro Miguel Lock
Cordillera (cuts)

Atlantic — Lake Gatun — Pacific

SEA LEVEL

Profile of Canal & Lake
Relationship of Sea, Lake, Locks and Cuts

Working Down the Gatun Lock

Although the Isthmus of Panama connects North and South America, the strip of land swings in a wide sweep so that actually it runs in an east-west direction. The Canal runs approximately from north to south. The mountains on the Isthmus run east and west, but they're much nearer the Pacific Coast than the Atlantic.

The idea, or plan, which the Canal builders had was very simple. They intended to dam rivers on each side of this mountain range (that on the north side drained to the Atlantic and that on the south slope ran to the Pacific) near their mouths. Thus two lakes were to be formed where none had existed before. The builders then intended to connect these two lakes by a very deep cut through the mountains which separated them. Locks placed in the dams would permit ships to be raised or lowered from the lakes to the sea. Lastly, channels would be dredged so that ships could sail from the oceans up to the locks.

While the concept of the Canal is most simple, its construction was unbelievably difficult. In addition to a vast number of engineering and designing problems, the Panama Canal presented one further difficulty. It was that of *size*. Nowhere on earth had man ever tackled anything so big before. The titanic hugeness of the Panama Canal project dwarfed everything else that had ever been attempted to alter the face of the globe and make it a more convenient and habitable place.

Today it is hard to visualize these staggering difficulties. Greenery and water cover the real works of the Canal. They hide its marvels, tend to make it seem a pretty run-of-the-mill thing.

All the measurements of the Canal are known, of course,

but they aren't very much use to us; they become meaning-less. What good is it to know that nearly *half a billion* cubic yards of earth and stone were excavated? Perhaps it stimu-lates the imagination a bit to realize that such an amount would build sixty-five pyramids the size of the largest in Egypt, or that if laid in a straight line it would build a wall the size of the Great Wall of China, extending from New York to San Francisco.

We know the dimensions of the locks—they are 1,000 feet long and 110 feet wide, but just how big is this? Try to imagine Cheop's pyramid. Each one of our lock systems, and there are twelve, contains as much *poured concrete* as the pyramid does of stone.

One of the commonest commodities during construction days was dynamite. We know how many tons of it were used, but this figure gives us very little idea of the enormous quan-tities of explosives needed. Think instead, of the tiny, cylin-drical holes drilled in the rock or the earth for each charge. If all these holes were laid end to end, they would make a neat little tunnel piercing our earth from side to side right at the equator.

You can look up all the data on Gatun Lake. Very accurate records are kept on depth, square miles of surface and so on. Instead, however, why not imagine a trip around its circum-ference in a dugout canoe? You will have to have an early start because not only will you lose a lot of time dodging the big 'gators, but you will also have a journey of over a thou-sand miles ahead of you.

There is no point in dwelling on mere bigness, but if we can get some idea of the size of these man-made things, then we will have an idea of what the Canal builders faced.

Colonel Goethals and his men seemed like pygmies, dwarfed by the mountainous task they had undertaken. They settled down to work—digging, blasting, pushing, pulling, picking up minute loads and, like industrious ants, depositing them elsewhere.

The job would take them years to accomplish.

Chapter 11

The basic foundation blocks upon which the entire concept of the Canal was created were the dams. These dams must hold back the water in the rivers, thus forming the lake over which the ships were to sail.

There were to be two dams—one on the Atlantic side and one on the Pacific. That on the Atlantic was the real problem.

A site was chosen at Gatun, about seven miles inland, where the valley of the Chagres narrowed. Halfway across the valley an island of solid rock jutted up from the floor. This was used to anchor the center part of the dam.

It was to be a mile and a half long, half a mile thick at the base and 100 feet wide at the top. A little arithmetic shows that the base is about twenty-five times as wide as the crest. The builders were taking no chance of its toppling over! The sides of the dam slope gently from the top in a curve that ends half a mile on either side.

Near one end, almost up against the hills, are the locks for lifting ships up or dropping them down to the sea. About in the middle, securely anchored to the little rock island mentioned, is the spillway and powerhouse. The powerhouse supplies electricity to run everything on the Canal Zone from the mules which haul ships through the locks to a waffle iron in one of the homes of the Zone towns.

The spillway performs an extremely important function. It controls the heights of the water in the lake, which must be held rigidly at a certain level. This level cannot vary more than two feet or the locks would have difficulty operating. During times of heavy rainfall, when the rivers are boiling full—especially the Chagres—the spillway is opened and excess water is allowed to escape to the sea. Lookout stations along the river, deep in the mountains, report to spillway operators the amount of rain, river height and its rate of flow. In this way it is known how much water can be expected long before its arrival in the lake, and the gates can be opened to forestall dangerous floods.

During the dry season, when smaller amounts of water come down the rivers, the operators close down the gates and restrict its escape.

Before work was started, every conceivable test as to the dam's feasibility was made. Holes were drilled into the earth and deep pits were dug—not only under where the dam would be, but at distances above and below it. The conclusion of the engineers was that the foundation was solid. The dam would hold. Next, a large model built to scale was constructed along the banks of the Chagres. It functioned beautifully. The crews were even able to calculate the amount of seepage which might be expected along the sides and underneath the completed structure.

When all was ready, when Colonel Goethals and his staff were completely satisfied, work started. The first thing that had to be done was to divert the Chagres River to one side.

The "toes"—the rock and earth walls built to do this—were themselves bigger than many other very large dams!

Trestles were erected, rails laid, and endless trains started bringing rock from the cuts and from quarries. Rock walls a third of a mile apart began to crawl outward across the valley.

The plan was to string these walls clear across the valley and then fill in the space between them with mud and clay. This mud and clay formed the "core" of the dam, and it came from the cuts on flat dump cars and from pipe dredges in the swamps below Gatun. As the water drained out of the core, oozing through the rock walls and flowing away to the sea, the clay settled and hardened. As it dried, it formed a solid mass, anchored to the rock walls above and below it, and to the hills on either side.

This work went on for more than nine years. Back and forth the trains scuttled, dumping their loads and returning for more. Against the immensity of the job, each load seemed like a tiny grain of sand, each grain piling bit by bit on top of the others. The task seemed futile—it could never be finished. However, slowly, imperceptibly, the walls and the core rose higher and higher with the passing years.

One bright morning, just as the work was getting under way, a newspaper reporter from the United States wandered over the site of the dam. He peered downward into one of the test borings and spied water—as it happened, from the rain of the night. Having nothing better to do he sent off a cable to his paper saying that Gatun Dam was located on an underground lake and was most unsafe.

The story was all over the United States the next day. Gatun Dam was on shaky foundations, the headlines screamed. It could not possibly hold. The greatest engineering blunder in history had been made at Gatun—and Americans were footing the bill.

The storm grew so loud that President Roosevelt appointed a team of nine eminent engineers to go to Panama for an inspection. They peered and they poked and probed and examined plans and samples of the borings. They agreed that the dam was perfectly safe. The damage had been done, however, and from then on the dam at Gatun and the entire high-level concept of the Canal were under constant and bitter criticism.

In 1908, it flared up again. Another reporter, overly anxious for a good story, wandered across the dam. Over that section which crossed the old French channel, he found a monstrous crack—a great slip in the core. He didn't know that this continually happened as the tremendously heavy weight of the rock and mud settled and slid and sunk, seeking a stable, solid foundation. His cable went off, and again the country was in an uproar! From New York to San Francisco, big black headlines announced the "disaster." The news soon spread abroad. Everyone was pleased, it seems, to herald the "failure" of the Americans in Panama.

London newspapers commented soberly. In Paris Bunau-Varilla shouted that the whole trouble was that the Americans had not located the dam in the proper spot, which was, naturally, that site picked out by French engineers long before!

Those who were still beating the drum for a canal in Nicaragua had a field day. Better give up the entire Panama project, they shouted. Write off the money, and then start over from scratch right where the canal should have been started in the first place.

In vain Colonel Goethals pointed out the truth—such slips were nothing; the dam was perfectly safe. He talked about his engineers and the tests they had made. He mentioned the model. Nobody cared about such calm words at a time like this! His words only added fuel to the fire. He was covering up, they said, saving his own skin. Far from the firing line, not knowing what was going on, the rear guard increased the uproar.

This time, no mere committee would do. Secretary of War Taft, backed by a full staff of congressional investigators and their experts, arrived on the Isthmus. They looked the situation over and asked a lot of questions—most of them pretty stupid. The story is still told on the Isthmus that when a certain senator saw the initials P.R.R. on a Panama Railroad coach, he stated in all seriousness that he never would have wasted time getting to the Isthmus by ship had he known that the Pennsylvania Railroad ran trains all the way down!

Again the verdict reached was that the dam was safe. The investigators simmered down and left. A bit fed up by now, the ditchdiggers were once again free to get on with the job. They had troubles of their own—real ones.

Pneumatic drills chattered, dynamite exploded, steam shovels clanked and bit into the earth. The dump trains never stopped rumbling and rattling over the trestles. Signal whistles screamed and cement buckets screeched on their trolleys overhead. Men's ears were dulled by the noise; nerves and muscles ached under the strain. No one man, or gang of men, could see how what they were doing fitted into any sensible, over-all pattern. The confusion was too great; the complexity and size of the task made it difficult to put any of the pieces together.

Eventually, however, order began to come out of the seeming chaos. A "whole" began to be discernible. Each individual task began to take on purpose. Gradually the dam, the locks and the spillway became a unit—assumed reality.

Days piled upon days, months on months and years on years. At last, in 1910, Major William Sibert, the engineer in charge at Gatun announced that it was time to block off the Chagres diversion channel and allow the lake to start filling. The rainy season was coming on and if this weren't done now, they would have to wait another year. The level of the lake had to be raised fourteen feet before it would flow over the spillway.

Trestles were built over the channel. The plan was to run trains out on the trestles and dump loads of rock into the river below faster than they could be washed away. On April 22 everything was ready. Hundreds and hundreds of loaded cars were on sidings at Gatun, and many more were backed up clear to Culebra, ready to make the dash.

They started dumping their loads, one after the other, as close as they could cram onto the tracks. As fast as whole trains were emptied, others rumbled out on the trestle to take their place. Thousands upon thousands of tons of rock were sent splashing down into the chasm. For a while all went well.

As the channel contracted, however, the flow of the current increased until great boulders weighing half a ton were whirled out and rolled downstream. The work became more and more difficult. Progress slowed. At last, when the channel shrank to a turbulent stream eighty feet wide and six feet deep, no more headway could be made. Rocks as big as a ton were tossed out like marbles. The number of the trains was increased, but there was no use. As fast as the loads were dumped, the water rolled them out.

Something had to be done immediately. Already in the mountains the thunder rumbled and ominous black clouds filled the sky.

There seemed no solution, until finally, as had happened so many times before, somebody remembered some old French equipment. Quickly two carloads of bent and twisted French rails were brought to Gatun, hauled out on the trestle and hurled into the water. The engineers hoped that the steel tangle would jam up against the trestle piers and hold the rocks. The trestle would go, or the dam would be built!

This did the trick. Slowly the rocks piled up, and slowly the rush of water was halted. At one time the whole thing very nearly was lost. The tremendous pressure built up against the trestle and retaining walls moved everything with a ghastly creak several feet downstream. Heedless of danger, the crews kept running their trains out on the wobbly tracks, dumping still more rock. Other brave men clambered down into the stream itself to reinforce the trestle girders. Suction dredges were quickly moved into hazardous positions and started pumping rock and mud and gravel back of the dam to give it strength. For a few very bad minutes the water in the lake lapped a scanty three feet below the top of the main dam wall.

There were many anxious days and frantic emergencies. Everything held, however, even though Major Sibert confessed later that it looked as though the Chagres were going to win. Within a month, the water in the lake had risen to the level of the spillway and commenced its roaring passage once more to the sea.

The crisis passed; the battle was won. Men returned to the work of completing the dam and the locks. The steady dumping of rock, the pumping of mud into the core went on monotonously. The structure rose higher and higher.

The Chagres had been tamed. In spite of the outcries from those who didn't know what they were talking about, the dam held and the locks were built.

On the Pacific side of the Canal, the problem of damming the Rio Grande River was nothing compared to the titanic project at Gatun. The mountains and valleys were narrow and deep, and the dam that was built was a mere gopher hill in comparison.

At Gatun, the eighty-five-foot difference between the lake and the sea was handled at one spot—with one gigantic dam and with the locks' three steps soaring upward in one continuous sweep.

On the Pacific side, the engineers decided to break this eighty-five-foot drop in two. Accordingly, two small dams were built, with locks in each one of them, and with a small body of water, Miraflores Lake, between them.

Chapter 12

If the dams are the bastions which support the Panama Canal, then the locks are their hearts.

Just what are they and how do they work? The difference in the levels between the oceans and the lake is eighty-five feet, and ships must be lifted and lowered this height as they make a transit. Ships are very heavy and bulky—some of them weigh seventy or eighty thousand *tons*. To move such a mass vertically might seem quite a problem.

Nothing is farther from the truth. The fact is that ships are simply floated up and down. The contrivance that does this job is a lock, and it is the simplest thing on earth.

You can do a little experiment if you like, but the principle is so obvious that you can easily visualize it.

Use a receptacle of some kind—anything that will hold water. A bucket or a pot will do very well. Put some water in the bottom of the bucket and float a toy boat in the water. Now hold the bucket under a tap or a garden hose and turn on the water. As the bucket fills, the boat rises. When the surface of the water, with the boat floating on it, reaches the top of the bucket, turn the tap off. The water has *lifted* the little boat perhaps a foot.

Now imagine you have a faucet in the bottom of your

bucket. If you open the faucet, the water runs out, the level in the bucket drops, and with it your boat. You have now *lowered* your toy a foot.

That's all there is to the principle of a lock. It doesn't matter how many feet high the bucket is—1, 10, 100 or more. The boat always goes up or down as you let the water in or out.

Suppose, now, there's nobody around to *put* the boat in the water, or perhaps it's too heavy for you to lift. Obviously, the boat has to *sail by itself* into the bucket.

You will now need a little watertight gate near the bottom of the bucket, on one side. Think now of a bathtub with a few inches of water in it. Open the faucet in the bottom of the bucket, and put it into the tub. Water will flow into the bucket through the faucet, until it reaches the level of that in the tub, then it will stop flowing. Now open the little gate, sail in your ship, and close the gate behind it.

Close the faucet in the bucket, turn on the tap of the tub and run water into the bucket. The bucket fills, lifting the boat.

To lower the boat back down, you must, of course, turn off the tap, open the faucet and let the water run out of the bucket. When it's down, you can open your gate and the boat sails out into the tub!

What do you do if you want the boat to be lifted up and then sail out the top of the bucket into a channel which is higher than the water in the tub, as it does in the Panama Canal?

Use the same bucket, only now, in addition to the little gate at the bottom, you install another one near the top. Then build a dam right across the tub and put the bucket tightly in it. On one side of the dam you put a few inches of water and on the other side you run it in until it is a foot or so deep. You can see that the dam and bucket must have a good tight fit between them or the water on the high side will leak out to the lower side.

Now sail in your boat, close the lower gate and faucet and fill the bucket from the tap. When the level is the same as that on the high side of the dam, turn it off. If you open your top gate now, the boat can sail right out onto the high water. To lower the boat from this high water side, just reverse the whole process.

In the Panama Canal, the seas on each side of the Isthmus correspond to the shallow water in the bottom of the tub. The lake in the middle of the Isthmus corresponds to the higher water level behind the dam in your tub. The bucket, of course, is the lock.

If you have to lift a ship a great height, such as the eighty-five feet at the Canal, then it will be more convenient to break your bucket, or lock, into several stages or steps. On the Canal, there are three steps. If this hadn't been done— that is, if they had tried to make it all in one gigantic eighty-five-foot leap—the machinery and the masonry would simply have been too big and heavy to manage.

When you filled your lock, you used a hose, or the tap in the tub. How are those locks filled on the Canal? Certainly nobody could stand there with a big fire hose running the water in.

The answer is that the water flows by *gravity* from the lake on the high side, through enormous pipes and tunnels in the walls of the locks into the closed chambers. When a ship is lowered, the water in a lock drains out by gravity, through other great pipes, into the sea below.

Such a system, called a hydraulic system, requires great care when it is in operation. The gates have to be opened and closed at just the right time, and the enormous valves, the "faucets" of your bucket, must be turned on and off at precisely the right moment. It would be disastrous to over-flow a lock chamber, or to empty it and leave a ship "stranded" on the bottom.

The whole process of filling and emptying the locks, clos-ing and opening the gates, is controlled by electricity. Men sit in the control towers, moving small switches and levers which actuate the necessary machinery. Through wide win-dows the operators look out and see what is happening at any moment. In addition, they have before them a small model on which the position of gates and the height of water is indicated at all times.

Every time a ship uses the locks, it takes water from the lake. Each year millions upon millions of gallons are lost in this way. Also, great amounts of water are lost by evaporation from the surface of the lake under the hot sun, through the hydroelectric plant at Gatun, and from seepage around the dams. Why doesn't the lake run dry? Because as fast as water is lost from the lake, it is replenished by the various rivers which run into it, particularly the mighty Chagres.

Panama is located in one of the rainiest parts of the world. If it weren't, such a system as that used at the Canal wouldn't work. Some of the downpours have been incredible during the ten-month-long rainy season. Once a record three and a half feet of rain fell in Colon in one month! During a damp afternoon in the old town of Portobelo, two and a half inches drenched the rain gauge in three minutes. The total for the night's "sprinkle" was over seven and one-half inches.

Rainfall such as this made it pretty certain that there would be enough water to operate the Canal and to generate electricity as well, provided, of course, that the water could be held back and saved for when it was needed. Detailed studies were made of rainfall and river flow over many years. The meticulous records kept by the French were enormously helpful.

There has always been plenty of water for Canal operation, but as ship passages increased, the problem became more and more of a worry. Recently a great dam, called Madden Dam, was built across the Chagres high in the mountains. Enough water is impounded in reserve to take care of any foreseeable demands.

Each step of each lock is built double. That is to say, each step consists of a *pair* of locks. This speeds up the whole locking procedure as it allows ships to go up and down at the same time. Water is also saved, because the huge tunnels under the locks connect the pairs crossways.

Vital parts of such a system are, of course, the gates. They have to be enormous in size and yet they must work smoothly and easily. They are built like double swinging doors coming together and closing in the middle.

Each of these doors is seven feet thick, sixty-five feet long and as high as a building six stories tall. To move such a ponderous and heavy steel structure called for the most clever and skillful design imaginable. They are hinged, of course, but on the bottom of each gate, rollers are fitted which run along tracks on the floor of the lock. Each gate also contains watertight, or buoyancy, compartments. These relieve some of the enormous weight.

To open and close the gate a five-foot "bull wheel," which operates an arm connected to each gate, is turned by an electric motor. The gates recess into the lock wall when they are open. Nothing must be left sticking out to interfere with the passage of ships.

The fit or joint in the middle where the two halves of the gates touch must be very tight and perfect, or water will leak out. This is known as a "mitre" fit. When the gates are swung out and the edges joined, another electric motor cinches up this mitre joint and drives it home to make it watertight.

If something calamitous should happen to the top gates, like breaking or jamming, then a great flood would pour out of the lake. Its flow would be so tremendous that it would wreck everything in its path, including the lower locks. Very likely it would drain all the water out of the lake because once started, there would be nothing to stop it.

To ward off such a disaster, huge emergency dams of steel are built to fit across the entrance of each top chamber nearest the lake. These gates are on pivots and contain giant sliding doors. Once swung into position, the doors would be closed one by one, until the rush of water was choked off.

To conserve the precious water, one more feature has been built into the locks. The main gates in each step are 1,000 feet apart. Few ships, however, are this long, so additional gates have been installed to make smaller chambers 400 or 600 feet long, for shorter ships. Naturally, the smaller the lock, the less water it takes to fill it.

There were many, many problems which had to be solved

when the locks were built. At Gatun, in the course of the centuries, the Chagres had deposited thick layers of silt over the valley floor. The tremendous weight of the concrete could cause the locks to settle down through this silt, so the whole sloppy mess had to be dug out right to bedrock. The laborers were in a huge and deep pit below sea level. The seepage from the ocean and the river made it a ghastly place in which to work.

The builders had to think of everything, and it's a wonder they dared tackle such a task. For example, not only the *downward* weight of the lock had to be considered. This country was so wet that seepage from many sources would most certainly work its way under the locks. The *upward* pressure on the floors had to be taken into account. If enough water gathered under a lock it might crack the floor, or even try to float the whole gigantic structure away, the way it might any watertight box! The floors were made thirteen feet thick, and each weighed the astonishing sum of 100,000 tons. Even this wasn't considered foolproof, and so the bottom of each floor was securely anchored down with steel rails spaced six feet apart and driven fifteen feet into the bedrock.

To supply the colossal amounts of concrete, a giant mixing plant was built right on the spot. A spiderweb of steel cables was spread overhead, carrying enormous buckets which delivered the mix to the forms. Some rock and gravel came from the cuts but most was brought in on barges from plants along the coast. A big rock-crusher was built in the old town of Portobelo. Sand was dredged and washed in a great plant located at another old gold port—Nombre de Dios. Tugboats and barges brought the material to Gatun, where unloading equipment delivered it to the always hungry mouth of the cement mixer.

On the Pacific side the same general scheme was followed with a few minor differences. Sand and gravel were taken from nearby quarries and from beaches along the coast. A cement mixer was also set up, but here, gigantic cranes running on tracks along the floor of the locks instead of overhead cables carried the mix to the forms.

The press at home, and all over the world, had for years been screaming about the "awful blunder" made at Gatun. On the Pacific side, a *real* blunder was made but it never reached the papers. Perhaps one reason for this was that at Gatun, the job, mainly because of the mighty dam, was more spectacular and attracted more reporters and visitors.

In the original plans passed by Congress, the location for the dams and locks on the Pacific side was much further out, near the sea. Soundings and borings had been made which seemed to assure firm foundations. As it turned out, these soundings were very superficial. John Stevens, long before Goethals, had protested bitterly the location chosen, but had been ignored.

Goethals too protested, but the site had been written into the authorizing act as law and could not be changed. Also, there was such a furor over Gatun at the time that nobody wanted to raise any more fuss. Talk about additional "mistakes" would have been very bad. Accordingly, Goethals started operations. Trestles were built and trains started dumping rock.

The blunder was so bad that the rock sank out of sight as fast as it was thrown in. At times it would rise high enough that tracks could be laid on it, but the weight of a locomotive caused it to ooze back down into the muck.

Such a location was impossible. Instead of the estimated ten feet of mud, Goethals now found out by really careful soundings that there were nearer seventy feet. If the locks *could* be built here, the cost would be outrageous. The chief engineer took it upon himself to notify his superiors, no matter how much of a storm might be raised. He explained the whole situation and included with his report an alternate plan which he and his engineers had devised. Secretary of War Taft sent the reports on to *his* superior, President Roosevelt. Fortunately, Congress was not in session. Roosevelt merely scribbled approval of the change and returned Goethals' new plans in the next outgoing mail! The change was announced soothingly, and explained as a mere relocation of dump lines! Actually, a major switch in the design of the Canal had been made. A fundamental engineering blunder had been committed, discovered and corrected with no fuss at all, and work proceeded with scarcely an interruption.

As men struggled in the mud and gumbo at each end of the Canal, another army of men battled the Isthmus elsewhere. The Atlantic Division had its own thorny, special problems as did the Pacific Division. The Central Division was something else. This great cut from Pedro Miguel to Gamboa was nicknamed Culebra, which means the *snake*. The name was well chosen and it stuck.

If the locks and dams tried men's patience and taxed their ingenuity to the limit, Culebra broke their hearts.

Chapter 13

A young engineer burst into the anteroom of Colonel Goethals' office. "I've got to see the colonel. Right away," he demanded.

The secretary looked up and sighed. Young men always had to see the colonel. And always right away. What emergency was this? Then the secretary corrected himself—there were no more emergencies—only crises. He tried to soothe the boy and calm him, but the effort was useless.

In the inner office Colonel Goethals heard the commotion and got up from his desk. He was glad to leave the hated paper work for a moment. Standing in his doorway he watched the agitated scene.

The young man spied him, rushed over. "Colonel," he said, "you've got to step outside. Come look. Quick."

Wonderingly, Goethals stepped out on the porch of his tin-roofed headquarters building, followed by an irked and mystified office staff.

The town of Culebra stood on the flat crown of a hill overlooking the cuts. Below it, stretching for miles in both directions, was the enormous gouge in the earth. Up out of it rose a deep, murmuring roar—a vast rumble of men and machinery, blended and confused by distance, smoke, steam, dust and fumes from dynamite explosions. Colonel Goethals and his staff had been looking at and listening to this scene for years.

Today there was a difference. A kind of breathless pause muted the sounds. The appearance of the hill was changed too. A huge chunk of the hill below the town had broken loose and was sliding ponderously downward. Colonel Goethals' office building was only feet from the edge of a precipice.

Goethals took a quick look at the scene. His eyes flickered and his jaw tightened slightly. He threw away a newly lighted cigarette and put a match to a fresh one.

"Tell them," he said briefly to his worried subordinate, "to dig it out."

Seventy-five acres of hill oozed ponderously downward at the rate of about three feet per day. No power on earth could have stopped it. It flowed into the "prism" of the cut, rose thirty feet up on the opposite side, burying and destroying everything in its path.

"Dig it out," Ferdinand de Lesseps had said back in 1882, and men had been digging almost without a stop since that time.

The French excavated 25 million cubic yards out of Culebra and finally came to a grinding halt. They had been defeated by this gigantic cut just as much as they had been beaten by their waste and graft.

In 1906 a special International Board of Engineers estimated that about 500,000 more cubic yards would have to be dug out. The dissenting minority members threw up their hands in horror, and *they* estimated that there were still about 55 million cubic yards to go—a hundred times as much!

The truth is that *nobody* really knew what Culebra could do, or what lay ahead.

By 1908 the American engineers were beginning to get some idea of the task. They upped the estimate to 78 million cubic yards. By the time they were through with the job in 1914—and Culebra was through with them—almost 103 million cubic yards had been dug out and carried away.

Thus did the Isthmus battle her despoilers. Again and again and again, as men patiently scooped this awesome rent out of the hills, she forced them back, like a valiant army repulsing invaders. As fast as crews dug out the earth and rock, she poured it back in, sometimes in a single night obliterating the work of months. Of the grand total of spoil taken out of Culebra, more than a quarter of it came from these counterattacks.

There were slides of all kinds, from roaring surface avalanches of rock to enormous, subterranean slips of the layers of greasy, soapy clay. There was also another kind, new to the engineers.

As the shovels bit their way deeper into the earth, the equilibrium of the mountains which had been established over millions of years was disturbed. The repose, or balance, of the surrounding hills was upset. Their incalculable weight caused them to settle, and in doing so, they squashed out rock and earth from beneath them. Frequently this tremendous pressure deep in the earth caused the floor of the cut to rise straight up in the air.

There was nothing that could be done about any of these cataclysmic movements. The floor of the cut had to be lowered if the job were to be finished. "Dig it out" was the only remedy. As fast as the slides came in they were dug out and hauled away. Each time it happened, the prism of the cut became wider and wider.

Naturally these slides were worse in the rainy season, but even when the ground was not wet, they continued. Old-timers tell of standing on the floor of the cuts and feeling the dry ground heave and buckle and rise beneath them, or of watching half a mountain ooze slowly and ponderously down into the prism, all the while giving off blinding clouds of dry, yellow dust.

Year after year the eternal task of digging went on. No end seemed in sight. Gradually the engineers realized that the opening date for the Canal would not be determined by the completion of the locks and dam at Gatun. Here, in Culebra, the final battle would be fought.

The basic tool was dynamite. A path nine miles long, wide and deep enough for ocean-going ships, had to be blasted through solid rock and packed clay, before the spoil could be removed. Over 60 million pounds of explosives were used. The chattering rock drills never ceased. The men took a two-hour lunch break on this job but not out of deference to the niceties of dining or of yielding to the Latin American custom of siesta. This time was to give the dynamite crews a chance to set and blow their charges. Again, in the evening, when the work day was over, blasting was done.

The loosened spoil was scooped up by great ninety-five-ton steam shovels. Each bite gulped up more than five tons. The operators made a fierce game of it, and competition among them was intense. Daily totals were most carefully kept. When suspicions of dishonesty arose or when skulduggery was suspected in the bookkeeping department, hot words and occasionally even fists flew. The all-time record for one shovel was 50,000 cubic yards in twenty-five working days.

As John Stevens had originally envisaged the cut, it was to be mainly a problem in transportation. And so it was. An extremely intricate rail system had been worked out to remove the mass of spoil as quickly as possible. In the narrow nine-mile gorge nearly 200 miles of track were laid. At times of peak activity over 115 locomotives hauled more than 2,300 spoil cars of every size and shape in and out.

About 160 loaded trains went out of the cut daily, and returned empty. This meant a total of 320 trains a day, or a train every minute and a half! There was untold confusion and unbelievable noise as these trains raced along a right of way about 300 feet wide, already cluttered with drills, steam shovels, and swarming with up to 10,000 men!

Nothing in the Canal Zone during construction days was moved by truck. For the shortest, even temporary hauls, ties and rails for trains were laid. Even the steam shovels in the cuts were on rails, and as they moved forward, the old tracks had to be torn up and new ones laid ahead of the shovel. An ingenious rail mover was developed which picked up an entire section—rails, ties and all—and moved it to the desired spot. Old-timers call the Canal Zone during construction days a "railroader's dream." Veteran engineers, real "hoggers" from all over the United States—men with coal smoke and steam in their blood—vied with each other for the chance to high-ball down the line of the Panama Railroad, through the cuts and over the continental divide. Dirt trains were given priority over everything else even on the main line. Passenger coaches, food trains, freight trains—they all had to pull to sidings and wait until the rumbling strings of flats had passed, en route to or coming from the dumping grounds.

Where to dump the spoil became a major problem. The Canal Zone only had an area of about 463 square miles, and more than half of this was taken up by Gatun Lake. Dump sites had to be chosen very carefully so that the spoil would not have to be moved a second time. Much of it went into the dam at Gatun. On the Pacific side, enormous amounts were dumped into the swampland near the Canal entrance, and on this reclaimed land, the future city of Balboa was to be built.

Colonel Goethals had put everything on a strict and tight time schedule. The order of each day was "hurry, hurry, hurry." Much time could be lost by using conventional methods on almost any job, and so to speed up the unloading of the flats, an entirely new system was devised. This was the famous Lidgerwood Unloader. Flat steel sheets were hinged to fall into the spaces between the cars. This made a smooth continuous platform from one end of the train to the other. When a train arrived at a dump, a blade, like the blade of a bulldozer, was pulled by a steel cable along the length of the platform, scraping it clean in a twinkling.

Those who worked in Culebra called it "hell's gorge," and it was an inferno in every sense of the word.

Before the growth of jungle covered the scars of the cut, they blazed and flashed in the sunshine with every eye-searing color in the spectrum. Early tourists, who didn't have to work down inside, were awed by what they saw, and they waxed poetically, ". . . the barbaric wealth of hues which blaze forth from these precipitous walls. Reds predominate —red of as deep a crimson as though Mother Earth's bosom thus cruelly slashed and scarred was giving up its very life's blood; red shading into orange, tropical, hot, riotous, pulsing like the life of the old Isthmus that is being carved away to make place for the new; red, pale, pinkish, shading down almost to rose color as delicate as the hue of a maiden's cheek, typifying perhaps the first blush of the bride in the wedding of the Atlantic and Pacific. Yellow too, from the brightest orange to the palest ochre, and blue from the shade of indigo—purple as royal as Ferdinand and Isabella ever wore, or the purple shades of the tropic sky, are there."

Apparently the sight was awesome and unforgettable, and as people tried to paint the picture in words, they were moved to flowery prose. Someone wrote: "He who did not see the Culebra Cut during the mighty work of excavation missed one of the great spectacles of the ages—a sight that at no other time or place was, or will be, given man to see. How it was best seen, many visits left me unable to determine. From the crest on a working day you looked down upon a mighty rift in the earth's crust, at the base of which pygmy engines and antlike forms were rushing to and fro without seeming plan or reason. Through the murky atmosphere strange sounds rose up and smote the ear of the onlooker with resounding clamor. He heard the strident clink, clink, clink of the drills eating their way into the rock; the shrill whistles of the locomotives giving warnings of some small blast, for the great charges were set off out of working hours when the Cut was empty; the constant and uninterrupted rumble that told of the dirt trains ever plying over the crowded tracks; the heavy crash that accompanied the dumping of a six-ton boulder onto a flatcar; the clanking of chains and the creaking of machinery as the arms of the steam shovels swung around looking for another load; the cries of men, and the booming of blasts. Collectively the sounds were harsh, deafening, brutal such as we might fancy would arise from hell were the lid of that place of fire and torment to be lifted."

In addition to the noise, the work, the sweat, the constant danger of accidents, the "little antlike forms" endured heat that might have rivaled the traditional temperatures of the furnaces of hell itself. During the dry season the rays from the blazing sun reflecting from the brilliant walls were trapped, and the pit became like an oven, almost unbearable for the sweat-soaked men working down in it. No one ever recorded temperatures in the bottom of the gorge, but above it, along the edges, where at least a few wisps of breeze moved, the thermometers rose as high as 132 degrees Fahrenheit in the sun at noontime.

Even the disturbed earth gave off heat and steam. Blasts hot enough to char a piece of wood came out of holes and cracks in the ground. For many these fumes were clear evidence that another blunder had been made: the Canal was surely being built on top of an active volcano! The geologists finally decided that the steam was caused by water vaporizing in the intense heat of friction as the earth writhed and slipped. The stinking, sulfurous fumes were from the oxidation of iron pyrites—ignited when air got to them. This underground heat added to the misery of the people working in the cuts, and they also were a real menace for another reason. Holes drilled in the sizzling earth by the dynamiters had to be cooled before charges could be placed, or premature explosions would result.

This clanking, boiling, witch's caldron was never completely quiet. When the workers had quit for the day, when the trains, the drills and the shovels had stopped rumbling, and when the final blasts had been set off, the cut settled down for the night. It was obscured in thick, swirling mists, and strange sounds, muted and weird after the clamor of the day, drifted up through the darkness. Supply trains rattled now and again through the cut, dropping off coal and other items. Men tended ailing machinery. Others kept steam up all night long on the shovels which must be ready to go in the morning. Over their lonely-sounding voices came the slam of furnace doors, the digestive rumble of boilers, the groan of pumps. Occasionally the clatter of the track-laying machine broke the vast silence briefly.

The years 1912 and 1913 were great years for tourists. Colonel Goethals always made them most welcome. He and his roughnecks were proud of the job they were doing. Forthright, honest publicity could do them no harm. Their greatest troubles in the past had been caused by people who did not understand what was going on. No one who came was disappointed. These were the years when the great works of the Canal were still naked and uncovered by water. They were also far enough advanced that their awesome size could be appreciated.

The welcome mat was out on the Panama Canal, and tourists flooded the Isthmus. They came from the United States and from all over the rest of the world. Congressmen, Presidents, royalty and just plain ordinary people came to see this fast-completing marvel of the twentieth century. No matter how cynical they might have been upon arrival, they always left awed and astounded by the spectacle. American steamship lines ran frequent tourist ships from New York and New Orleans. The French Line, the Hamburg-American Line, and the Royal Mail Line all scheduled weekly arrival of liners from Europe, and each was jammed with expectant sightseers.

The huge Tivoli Hotel, in the Canal Zone at Ancon on the Pacific side, enlarged its dining room to serve 600 people at one sitting. Rubberneck trains shuttled back and forth across the Isthmus and along the brow of the cuts, dodging thundering spoil trains. Barge and launch expeditions were run on regular timetables; a great public exhibition, complete with models, was set up in an enormous warehouse-turned-theater. The tourists were free to roam at will, wherever they chose, except in certain ultra-dangerous spots, such as on cranes, inside lock tunnels or aboard operating machinery. The organized tours were the best way to see the whole works. The project was so vast and apparently so disjointed and disconnected that it was difficult to make heads or tails of it without the services of the professional "explainers."

Word had gone out from the boss that nothing was to be left undone to make the visitors happy. The handling of visitors—their transportation, their feeding, care and education—was as thoroughly planned and organized as the building of the Canal itself. The show was a great one. Old-timers liken it to a circus midway, complete with spielers, barkers and soda pop.

As time went on, the public spotlight shifted from Gatun, and the locks at Balboa, to Culebra. Instinctively people realized that here the final and most dramatic battle with the Isthmus was taking place.

Veterans of the cut went crazy, took to drink, or broke under the strain. Major Gaillard, the engineer in charge of the cut, cracked and eventually died. The official name of the passage became Gaillard Cut, in his honor, but the old name of the snake—Culebra—is hard to dislodge.

The years passed. Gradually the locks and dams neared completion, and men were putting on the finishing touches, such as railings on the stairways and electric lights. Presidents came and went. Roosevelt's two terms expired. William Howard Taft was elected, served a term and then was defeated by Woodrow Wilson.

Still they dug it out in Culebra.

Chapter 14

Statistics and comparisons help to visualize the size and complexity of the job of building the Panama Canal. However, an understanding of the mechanical marvels of the Canal is only a part of the tale. Back of everything there is something more. Men. Only men can clothe a story with the flesh and blood of life.

For long, peak periods of employment, over 50,000 men were on the payroll. To maintain such a formidable army in the face of deaths, rejections, turnover and many other reasons, more than 250,000 employees had to be recruited. Those selected streamed toward the Isthmus from half the civilized world. They came from America, and they also came from faraway Greece, from France, England, Ireland, Spain, Italy and Scandinavia. They came too by the tens of thousands from the islands of the Caribbean—Barbados, Jamaica, Tobago, St. Thomas, St. Kitt, Bermuda, Curaçao, Martinique, Trinidad and many others.

This vast army of workers was divided into two categories, the Gold Roll and the Silver Roll. These names came from the custom of paying one group of men in gold coins and another in silver coins. No checks or paper money were used, as they deteriorated too quickly in the hot, moist climate.

The Gold Roll was made up almost entirely of Americans. This was the administrative and technical group; these were the men with the know-how. The Silver Roll was entirely non-American. This was the laboring group; these were the men who worked with their muscles. This Gold-Silver separation swiftly developed into a strict and rigid caste system. Whatever its original intent, it ultimately became a division based on race. White Americans were on one side, and all others (although overwhelmingly non-American Negro), were on the other.

The lines of this separation spread far beyond the original and simple classifications based upon method of payment, type of work done or salary. It came to dictate every aspect of life on the Canal Zone. The "Silvers" and "Golds" lived in different towns; they used different drinking fountains and toilets; they used different commissaries, went to different movies, ate in different messes.

During the construction years, when quite truthfully, the only skilled personnel available were American, this system caused little trouble. In later times, the stranglehold which it had over the entire Zone was a bitter thing and caused much friction.

Thus from its very beginning, the Zone tended to become a tiny closed corporation of different cultures. Those who came here to live and to work were lonely. They brought with them from their distant homes strong memories and a fierce pride. When they walked off the ships down the gangplanks they found that their countrymen who had preceded them were organized and waiting with open arms. Filipinos welcomed Filipinos, Greeks welcomed Greeks, Spanish greeted Spanish and various groups composed of West Indians awaited newcomers from their home islands.

The Americans, too, stuck together. On every level—social, cultural and professional—they banded with each other to the exclusion of everyone and everything "foreign." There were individual exceptions, of course, but by and large rare indeed was the American who let himself be slightly "contaminated" by the flavor and excitement of the nearby Latin-American countries. Only a tiny handful ever bothered to learn even a dozen words in Spanish. They arrived on the Isthmus as small-town Americans. Transplanting their home culture to their new home, they remained exactly as they arrived.

Within these rigid patterns, life functioned very smoothly and tranquilly on the Zone. The job to be done was overpowering. Its demands were enormous—too great to allow time for deep animosities to develop. Men had come to build the Panama Canal; the highest to the lowest felt a sense of pride and hope for accomplishment as the long task slipped into high gear.

The work was dangerous, there was deaths, and the Isthmus of Panama exacted even more than her share of blood from these new invaders. Men were caught in great gears and cogs and pulleys; they were brushed from trestles by rattling freights, washed overboard from barges at sea. They were swept into swiftly flowing torrents of concrete, trapped in sickening slides, buried in deep pits, torn apart in premature explosions. Death came in hundreds of ways to men of all races, but it came most of all to the ubiquitous West Indians, whose strong backs, courage and cheeful willingness contributed so much toward making the Canal possible.

The Panama Canal, during the construction years, killed about five hundred men a year. Hospital cars rattled at the end of every train; in the cemeteries fresh graves were always ready and waiting. There are no monuments to the memory of all those who died—except possibly the Big Ditch itself.

If some came to the Isthmus and found death, many, many others came to find opportunities and a life which was good and sweet. Many—a very great many—even came to get married!

Uncle Sam at one time was accused of running the biggest matrimonial agency in the world. New brides arrived by the scores! They came on every ship to sweeten the lives of tropical tramps and other assorted Canal roughnecks. On one memorable day, ten fluttery, blushing brides arrived on one ship and all were married within twelve minutes after debarking. Colonel Goethals and his men prided themselves on getting things done in a hurry those days.

These "honeymoon" ships provided many lighter moments for the nearly all-masculine population of the Zone. The story is told of one balky miss from Kansas who refused to marry the boy until he got out of the flour sack he was wearing! In the early days there were shortages of nearly everything, including lightweight linen for clothing. Somebody discovered that flour sacks, bleached and cleaned, could be tailored into excellent suits. Many an old-timer today still proudly cherishes his flour-sack suit, something perhaps like an old school tie. Such mementos are only brought out on gala occasions or when it is necessary to impress some upstart newcomer.

The young lady didn't know about such traditions, and her weeping could be heard from one end of the dock to the other. The minister was finally able to explain; she and her sweetheart were married, but she never lived the incident down.

Flour sacks or not, the bachelor-filled Canal Zone was a happy hunting ground for the girls. The young Canal male, whether he was an engineer, a bookkeeper or a machinist, was top-grade husband material.

As a young bachelor, one of the colonel's boys, he never had it so good. He was advancing himself professionally by working on the most important job in the world. His pay was 25 per cent over what he could make at home on a similar job. He received forty-two days a year paid vacation plus another thirty days of sick, or recuperative, leave. He had no room rent to pay, no medical bills, no lighting bills, no heating bills. His clothing requirements were at a rock-bottom minimum, and for eighteen to twenty dollars a month he could eat his fill. True, he worked very hard and was dirty, sweaty and muddy most of the time. This he didn't mind; it was part of the excitement of the job. There was very little opportunity to spend money, and he was saving his salary and accumulating a nice bank account.

There was only one problem. The typical young man was lonely. As he mulled the matter over in his mind, often in his drab bachelor room which he shared with two or three other young ditchdiggers, just as lonely and dirty and tired and grumpy as he, he began dreaming about a vision in cool tropic white welcoming him home at the end of each day to a vine-and-bougainvillea-covered cottage. The more he thought about it, the more reasonable the whole idea seemed. Why shouldn't he be married?

The letters streamed northward in an ever-increasing flood

to sweethearts in the States, urging them to catch the next boat. When the nervous brides began arriving, they found that the glowing proposition had in no way been misrepresented.

Of course at first, married quarters were at a premium, but Colonel Goethals was not the man to allow this to remain out of control. Although no doubt exaggerated, the story is told on the Isthmus that at one time he had so many clamoring newlyweds on his hands that finally he stopped work on the Canal and turned everybody to building quarters.

When a young couple finally moved into a place of their own, life began to glow. Nearly everything except food was free. On the list were such things as rent, light, janitor service, distilled water, fuel, medical and hospital care. The little flat was furnished free by the omniscient Canal Commission. All that the bride and groom had to buy were bedclothes and china. For these items the thoughtful Commissary Division had scoured the world and offered the best at astonishingly low prices. Later, when children began to arrive, they too shared in all this bounty.

The young wife had never seen anything like this before! Her little flat was kept more or less tidy by a grinning and cheerful maid whom she paid (out of her own pocket) ten or fifteen dollars a month. In the commissaries she found that her coupons would buy everything from French perfume to Irish linen to English chinaware; from Danish delicatessen tidbits to fresh fruits from Peru, to choice Argentine filet mignon. The colonel lamented that his Commissary Division had trouble getting rid of beef forequarters. Nobody wanted to eat these lesser meat cuts!

When friends came to dinner, the meal was apt to be lavish—all the way from Chesapeake oysters to roast to strawberry shortcake. All the guests had also received the same commissary shopping list and could predict quite accurately what they might be served, which somewhat took the fine edge from the fun of having company.

The young couple faced up to a formidable array of outside entertainment. There is little doubt that Zonians were among the best-organized and joiningest people in the world.

The Y.M.C.A. and the government clubhouses—the "clubbies" so fondly remembered by everyone who has lived and worked on the Zone—were the centers of much of the social life. In addition, the number of private clubs and organizations was quite beyond belief. There were States' Societies, Old-Timer's Clubs, Strangers' Clubs, Chagres Societies, poetry groups, theater groups; the list was endless, and all of them flourished happily. Rare was the week end when a Zonian didn't have to decide among a baseball game, a picnic or two, a card game, a fair, a tug-of-war match, a dance or some other function. If he didn't have such a choice he was either a snob or a confirmed and hard-bitten stick-in-the-mud.

Life for those on the Silver Roll was not quite so idyllic as it was for those on the Gold Roll. The Silver employees were not cared for quite so solicitously.

The bachelor Silver men slept in great huge barracks and dined in enormous messes, sometimes standing and sometimes with the luxury of tables. Each nationality was served its special food preferences, and frequently this food, and the quarters, were inspected by their country's consul in the Republic of Panama. Thus the Italians had their spaghetti and red wine; the Spanish their *garbanzos;* the West Indians their rice and salted codfish. For them, too, there were many things on the free list—quarters, medical care, light, water and so on—all of which they needed on wages only a fraction of those paid on the Gold Roll.

The Silvers also were infected with the organizing fever. The men were banded into jealous, lonely little segments which clung tenaciously to the music, food and customs of far-off homelands. The West Indians were the greatest joiners of all. The socializing among these gregarious people was enormous; a man might have several important meetings in one night, and changing from one gorgeous uniform to another could present quite a problem. Their parties ranged all the way from formal dances with elegant music and food, to black magic, voodoo ceremonies performed deep in the forest by the bank of a swamp, with a demijohn of good native rum to keep the evil eye at a distance.

Early, Silver wives began arriving, as often as not without the benefit of formal matrimony. Some of the Silver families lived in married quarters—a pair of small rooms in an enormous barracks, with cots and convenient space to set up charcoal braziers on the wide balconies. Others preferred the independence of a tiny tarpaper and tin shack which a benevolent commission allowed them to build on a little island somewhere, or at the edge of swamp or jungle.

For those on the Silver Roll, life was not easy. The work was hard and dangerous. The pay was low. There was no retirement, save at the discretion of the Canal commission. Many of those who came to work on the "big job" quit and went home. Largely, however, they stayed. For most of them, life in many respects was better than that which they had left behind. In addition, nearly to the last man, they shared in the general pride and thrill of accomplishment working on the most important construction project in the world.

For Americans, the solicitude and the paternalism, no doubt had its very pleasant aspects. They were, however, stripped clean of one great birthright. They had no voice in governing themselves. They could not even say where they would live or how much they could afford for quarters or what kind of furniture they would own. The government, in this case the Canal Commission, did everything for them, decided everything for them.

The social strata were as rigidly fixed as those of any British colonial outpost at the height of the Empire's glory. Only before the magnitude of the work were these strata erased. Elsewhere a man's status and his way of life were inflexibly controlled by his position on the payroll. A salary of $275 a month entitled him and his family to a few more square feet of living space, or perhaps another pillow or rocking chair, than did a salary of $250.

The benevolent head of this enormous, paternalistic, and *extremely* hard-working, beehive was, of course, Colonel Goethals. The fear with which his arrival had been greeted was soon turned to admiration, to respect and, finally, to enormous affection.

He was a very fine engineer; he was a most strict boss and father, but he was also a kindly all-seeing, all-knowing humanitarian in the very finest and broadest sense. People did what he told them to do, and no fooling about it either, but he never told them to do anything which was against their best interests. His position on right or wrong was inflexible; the decisions and the justice which he meted out were rarely questioned; they rarely needed to be questioned. All-powerful, he ruled his complex and bustling kingdom of Canal works, schools, railroads, commissaries, courts, fire departments, clubhouses and hospitals. From his decisions there was no appeal. What he said settled the matter, and an occasional erring Zonian found this out when he thought he had gotten a raw deal on some matter and suddenly began demanding his rights. He didn't have any!

Goethals' responsibilities were, of course, tremendous. He worked as hard as, and probably much harder than, any other man on the Canal Zone. The variety of problems in which he was involved was incredible; the load which he carried would have crushed a lesser individual.

His mornings were invariably spent in the field. He covered the job from one end to the other in his famous Yellow Peril, a brightly painted motor scooter which ran on rails. He bobbed up in the most unexpected places, asking questions, taking his workers to task. His afternoons and evenings were devoted to planning, to administrative matters and paper work in general.

In spite of his very full days, Colonel Goethals was also personally available to any worker at any time. On Sundays he held court in his offices and dispensed informal, but most authoritative, justice to anyone with troubles. With good humor, much wisdom and understanding, he settled all kinds of problems. These sessions have been described as similar to the levies which Louis XIV of France used to hold under the trees at Versailles.

The "Colonel," as he was called by high and low, was a good, dedicated soldier and a fine man. He never spared himself, whatever the task or problem brought to him. His purpose in life was to finish his assigned task as quickly and economically as possible. If $50,000 a month could be saved by shaking out cement bags more thoroughly, he would see that it was done. If the plans and location for a gigantic set of locks were faulty, his own light, as well as those of his engineers, would burn late until the changes were made. Colonel Goethals poked his fingers into every aspect of work and life on the Canal Zone. He kept his Silver employees reasonably content; he pampered his Gold employees shamelessly. He made them all behave.

He did all these things because he most certainly believed that by so doing, the Canal would be completed that much sooner. Perhaps he was right. Under his benevolent but authoritative hand, the dirt really flew!

Chapter 15

The "grand opening" of the Panama Canal was on August 15, 1914, and was marked by the official transit of the venerable SS *Ancon*. Actually, this was the triumphant climax to a long series of lesser triumphs. The true "opening" of the Canal was done in bits and pieces and spread out over a year.

The first hint that the construction years were drawing to a close took place at 4:30 in the afternoon of May 20, 1913. Operating on what was to be the deepest level of the cuts and coming from opposite directions, two snorting, clanking steam shovels ate their way through a tangle of dirt and rock. They ground to a halt and seemed to eye each other with deep satisfaction. They had a right to be content. After four centuries, a pathway had been cut down to grade across the Isthmus. Trains screeched to a halt. Sweat-stained men threw their hats into the air and cheered themselves hoarse; every whistle in the cut added to the din. Photographers recorded the great event.

By August of the same year, the work had very nearly come to a head. The time was drawing near to let water into the Canal.

The Pacific side was first. A gigantic dam to keep the sea

out had been built across the channel a mile below Miraflores Locks. This dike was drilled and about twenty tons of dynamite were set. So that everybody could join in the fun, the colonel set the date for the big blast on a Sunday—the thirty-first.

Long before time for the explosion—9:30 in the morning —thousands of people had gathered. They made a gala picnic out of it and were well equipped with basket lunches and umbrellas.

Right on time the dynamite went off with a satisfying roar, tearing a gigantic hole in the dike. The people settled down with their refreshments to await the next act, the coming of high tide at noon.

The water on the Pacific side comes in fast, with a rush. Now it poured like a mighty Niagara over the debris of the dike, a height of about six feet. Faster and faster it came, sweeping everything in a churning torrent before it. Soon the channel was swept clean as a whistle and the waters of the Pacific lapped quietly against the closed gates of Miraflores Locks.

Two days later the dike across the channel at Gatun on the Atlantic side was removed. This was less spectacular, as a movable span had been operating in the dam for months and the waters on each side of it were already equal in height.

On September 24, the seagoing tug *Gatun* quietly locked up from the sea into Gatun Lake. The trip took about two hours. Quite understandably, everyone was a bit nervous and overcautious and careful. The transit "up the stairs" was a complete success, and those voices of doom which had been prophesying for years that the great triple-stepped locks would never work were at last silenced.

The colonel had decided that the final excavating in Culebra would be done by dredges rather than by steam shovels. This meant, of course, that water must be let into the cut. For weeks the Army of Panama had been retreating. Broken-down machinery, worn-out locomotives, drills, track and endless other equipment were hauled out. Eventually the cut was empty and silent for the first time in years.

Three years before the engineers had dammed off the Chagres diversion channel. Over all this time the lake was slowly filling. An enormous dike had been built at Gamboa to keep this water out of the cut while the steam shovels were at work. The first order of business was to get rid of that barrier.

Huge culverts had been installed under the dike, and these were now opened. Torrents of brown muddy water flowed through the culverts from the lake into the cut. Meanwhile a gigantic slide—the granddaddy of them all—had come down in the cut at a place called La Cucuracha—the cockroach! The water could only flow as far as Cucuracha, but when it had risen to the level of that in the lake, it was planned to blow both Cucuracha and the Gamboa dike in a pair of mighty blasts. October 10 was set for the big day. It was an unofficial holiday. Not one person on the Isthmus would want to miss this occasion. Special trains and boats took thousands of celebrants to the scene.

When everything was set, President Wilson pressed an electric button in the White House. A relay snapped in far-away Panama, and with an earth-splitting roar the charge at Gamboa went off. Tons of water and mud were tossed high into the air. Everybody agreed it was one of the most magnificent sights ever seen on the Isthmus. It must have been tremendous, because these were people not easily awed by any run-of-the-mill dynamite explosion.

The lake was six feet higher than the water in the cut, and so a great wave swept down the channel. Like Hawaiians riding surfboards, a native in a dugout and Americans in two launches rode its crest, all headed for Pedro Miguel. They got only as far as Cucuracha, which didn't even quiver under the surge of the big wave.

In a final fit of stubbornness, the Isthmus resisted every attempt to dislodge the slide. Unheard charges of dynamite were set off—charges so heavy that the Canal line for miles was shaken. Houses rocked on their foundations, dishes clattered. The mud and rock flew into the air and fell back more tightly packed than ever. Cucuracha was firm and determined to hold out.

A flotilla of dredges had been brought up from the Atlantic, through Gatun Locks, across the lake and into the cut as far as the slide. They dipped their snouts in the mud and industriously started chewing. It was slow work, though, and the harassed engineers tried everything they could think of to get the water across the slide so more dredges could be brought up from the Pacific. Nothing worked.

At long last, as though finally tamed and relenting, the Isthmus herself came to the aid of these stymied humans. Heavy, steady rain fell throughout an afternoon and a night. The Chagres began to flood. In three days the level of the lake had risen three feet. A small trench was shoveled out by hand across Cucuracha, and a little stream of water began to flow across it. Deeper and deeper the water bit into the mud.

The stream increased to a torrent, flushing rocks, clay and mud before it. Soon the dry section was filled with water to the end of the cut. Dredges were locked up from the Pacific and went to work.

By April 1, 1914, the channel was deep enough that an ancient French crane boat, the *Alexander la Valley* made the *first transit* from ocean to ocean. Next, a battered and beaten old tug, the *Mariner,* made the trip, hauling a pair of barges.

From now on, things happened fast. The Canal was in business. Its first customer was the American Hawaiian Steamship Line. For years this company had brought sugar and canned pineapple from Hawaii to the Isthmus of Tehu-antepec in Mexico for transshipment across to the Caribbean, where the cargo was loaded on other ships and taken to New York. The SS *Alaskan* of this company presented herself in the Bay of Panama and asked Colonel Goethals for help. The ship had 12,000 tons of cargo aboard, and because of the disruption of traffic across Mexico, she had been unable to unload. The colonel gladly welcomed this first client, and the pineapple and sugar were lightered across. Regular lighter service between the two oceans was quickly established and by June 10, 1914, the Commisison Auditing Department proudly announced that the Canal had shown its first profit—a modest $7,356.12!

On the eighth of June, Goethals was ready to try a regular ocean-going steamship. He chose the *Allianca* an old Panama Railroad freighter. She locked up to Gatun Lake and back down again without a scratch. The trip of the *Allianca* brought to focus a battle which had been quietly raging for years: How do you handle a big ship in the locks? How were

Two Way Traffic at the Gatun Locks

the pilots to control her? How do the mule operators co-ordinate? The lockage was made very slowly and very care-fully. Everything worked perfectly.

Now the time had come to make a formal announcement to the world. August 15 was the date set for the first official transit.

Goethals needed a dress rehearsal. The *Cristobal,* sister ship of the *Ancon,* was in port and was selected. She made the trip safely, but not without incident, on August 3. Many bugs were still to be ironed out in the handling of such a large vessel in the locks. The time up to August 15 was spent in concentrated practice.

On this first voyage, a few dignitaries and old-time em-ployees made the trip. One passenger deserves special men-tion. It was none other than Monsieur Bunau-Varilla.

August 3 was the same day that World War I started in Europe, and Bunau-Varilla learned the news while en route on the Canal. He solemnly stated:

During the . . . years which lapsed from 1885 to 1914, two ambitions filled my brain and heart. What I desired more than any other material or moral satisfaction was, first, to see the immortal creation of the French genius at Panama finally com-pleted for the utility and service of civilization; second, to see France washing the slate of history with Prussian blood. . . . By an extraordinary coincidence the glorious war of 1914 began on the very day that the first ocean steamer passed from the Atlantic to the Pacific.

"French genius"—and that of a lot of other people as well —finally made the words of Bunau-Varilla about the Canal a glorious reality.

A grand celebration for the formal opening on August 15

had been planned, including a gigantic naval parade of merchant and warships through the Canal. In view of the somber, agonizing bloodletting under way across the seas, the party was canceled. No one was in a mood for much jubilation.

The *Ancon* made her inaugural trip on August 3, but the fiesta was a relatively private one. The only guests were those who had labored so long and so hard to make the Canal a reality—the living, and the ghosts of all those who had died over the centuries.

Chapter 16

That long-ago day on August 15, 1914, when the battered and dented *Ancon* glided smoothly through the ships anchored in the roadsteads of Colon and Balboa, was one of real triumph. That day had seen a miracle—a man-made miracle. Once again man had demonstrated his ability to overcome the physical barriers which had separated him from his fellow men.

When the Suez Canal was completed, the interminably long voyage around the Cape of Good Hope was eliminated. All of Europe was easily accessible to the Orient. A very huge part of the Pacific, however, was still cut off from the rest of the world. The people who lived far to the north in the Orient, to the south in Australasia, and those along the entire western shoreline of North and South America were still isolated. Any way a ship might choose to go from the Atlantic—via Suez, the Cape of Good Hope, or through the Straits of Magellan—to the Pacific, she still faced a long, long voyage.

When the Panama Canal was opened, such a voyage was shortened tremendously. The 13,135-mile trip from New York to San Francisco via the Straits of Magellan shrunk to a mere 5,562 miles. In the old days of sailing ships, with low wages, low upkeep, and no fuel bills to pay, distance was of little concern. It didn't matter if a voyage took six months or a year to complete. Today, however, distance means time, and time translates directly into money. Each day that a ship is at sea is tremendously costly. Vessels must make their voyages quickly, unload and load quickly, and be on their way. The inauguration of the Panama Canal meant that the people inhabiting the shores of the Pacific Ocean could be served by regular and frequent steamer service; in a very real sense they "joined" the rest of the world.

Like the Panama Railroad before it, the Canal was needed so badly that it was a going concern even before it was finished. Over the years the number of vessels using the Canal has steadily increased. Tolls remain the same as those set in 1938 in spite of plans to raise them. Shipping interests howled so loudly that the matter of the increase was "put off for further study." Rates are seventy-two cents per ton for ships in ballast, ninety cents a ton for laden ships, and fifty cents a ton for warships.

In 1951 the waterway took in $25 million in tolls. In 1952 it rose to $30.5 million and in 1953 a record-breaking $37.5 millions were collected. Over that last year, other services increased the total income to $107,457,716, and the enterprise showed a net profit of $7,200,963. "Other services" are many and include the railroad, the sale of oil, water and supplies, dry-docking and ship repair facilities, rental of land, and so on.

The Canal has not only brought much good to mankind, but it has also been a success financially. However, as with all things, the passing of time has brought problems and changes.

The Zone is no longer the Utopia that it once was for American employees. A parsimonious Congress has nibbled away at many of the fringe benefits which they used to enjoy. No longer is the Panama Canal Company the generous, ever-doting father. Employees now pay rent, income taxes, fees for medical and hospital services, and so on. These fees are not high but they have nevertheless tended to reduce the over-all living standard.

Many a penny-pinching congressman, anxious to make an "economy" name for himself, has introduced bills which in one way or another have nibbled at the livelihood of Zone employees. These employees are particularly vulnerable to such tactics, as they do not have congressional representation themselves. In recent years, they have found a voice, however, and have been demanding their rights through lobbies in Congress, labor unions and so on.

The position of the Gold Roll employee has thus changed greatly since construction days. Our policy toward those on the Silver Roll also has changed. There are new trends and new attitudes on the Isthmus. This is all to the good because the Canal Zone is in a sense a showcase, a little bit of America set down in the heart of a foreign country. Quite aside from the basic injustice of the old system, our country could not forever permit a wretched, securely entrenched Jim Crow society to exist there. The old hateful words of Silver and Gold have been abolished. The rigid caste strata are dissolving slowly. Pay differentials are being equalized. Opportunities for higher pay jobs in the skilled categories are bit by bit opening up for all, on the basis of skill alone rather than on nationality or color. Our early attitudes made us many bitter enemies, but today as we conduct our affairs there with more foresight and understanding, the tensions are lessening.

The least that can be said about our relations with the Republic of Panama is that they are varied and complex. Often they have been bitter and angry.

Panama is a prosperous little nation with a general standard of living higher than most Latin American lands. Undoubtedly a great part of this prosperity is due to the Canal. The direct benefits are easy to calculate. We paid Panama $10,000,000 outright when we started the Canal; the yearly rental was to be $250,000. This was later increased to $430,000, and in 1955 it was increased to $1,900,000.

The indirect benefits are enormously greater and likewise much more difficult to establish. Although Panama ultimately footed the bill for the work, we nevertheless cleaned up the two big cities in the republic, provided good sewage facilities, good water, garbage service, got rid of malaria, yellow fever, cholera and typhoid. Ships and tourists passing through make many purchases in the republic. The Panama Canal Company buys cement, cattle, sugar and other items from Panamanian businessmen. Zone employees, American soldiers and sailors, and crewmen from merchant ships each year spend large sums of money "across the line." All these things contribute greatly to Panama's financial health.

However, there is another side to the coin. Panamanians resent bitterly the point of view of too many Americans, particularly those expressed by their neighbors in the Zone, that we "gave" them their independence, or that we "own" their country, or that they would starve to death without the Canal.

They resent the hated Gold-Silver system. Their position

has always been an inferior one because, regardless of education, a Panamanian could only find Zone employment on the Silver Roll. They have felt as aliens on "their own soil."

Panama has never forgiven us for our precipitate haste in signing the original Canal treaty with a man who wasn't even a Panamanian citizen. In spite of all the high-sounding phrases, the truth is that Bunau-Varilla was a real opportunist and did very well for himself and his pocketbook. His name is still a hated one, and the whole subject is still a sharp thorn in our good relations with the Republic.

Supernationalists in Panama, and there are many of this volatile breed, demand nothing less than complete sovereignty over the Canal and the railroad. They point to Egypt and Suez and hint darkly of local Nassers. Most Panamanians, however, believe that the best future of their country lies in patient negotiation with the "Colossus of the North" and are content to see improvements come about gradually. The original treaties, once thought inviolable, have undergone many changes—most of them in the interests of fair play and better relations with Panama. Both governments are coming to understand the wise words of one of the republic's best presidents: "Treaties are written by men. Only God makes eternal things."

Meantime, the importance of the Canal increases almost daily. Many very serious problems, quite apart from human ones, concerning the future of the Panama Canal face our government. They must be solved soon.

Theoretically, the Suez Canal is an "international" canal, and in times of war is available to the ships of any nation—warships or merchant vessels. The Panama Canal is a "private" canal. It belongs to us. In wartime it is open only to our own ships and those of our allies. We defend it and patrol its approaches to see that this is so. This seems reasonable and yet many thinking people say this is wrong. They say that control of a great interocean waterway, which benefits all mankind, should not be in the hands of any one nation.

On the other hand, military men say that the canal is vital for the defense of our country. They say it must be available to us, and to us alone, when the time comes to assemble equipment and soldiers. Those who argue the other way state that the canal is *so* important that surely it must be high on the priority list of any enemy, and that because it is so vulnerable, especially to modern, highly accurate rocket weapons, it could easily be destroyed and be of no use to anyone. They claim that the only way to protect the waterway, which is of such great benefit to all men, is to internationalize it.

About one thing there is no argument: the Panama Canal has about reached the limits of its capacity!

Today it can handle all the ships which slide past the breakwaters and head for the locks. Very soon, though, the breaking point will be reached. In about fifteen years the canal will have to start turning ships away.

The Big Ditch holds her own now only by stretching to the very limit. Never designed or built to accommodate so many customers, the canal is literally glutted with traffic. The locks are the big bottlenecks. Locks need eight minutes to fill with water; a ship takes fifteen minutes to pass from one to the next. No matter how pressed, the operators can do very little to decrease this time. The greatest care must be taken to avoid gargantuan traffic jams that could pile ships up for miles back through the dangerous cuts into the lake. Yearly each set of locks has to be put out of commission for a thorough overhaul, and this further slows down and complicates the traffic tangle. Powerful electric lights and beacons have been installed to lengthen the dawn-to-dusk transit day, but this is only a stopgap measure.

The locks today are even too small! Three times during construction, plans were made which enlarged the chambers, but in spite of this, many ships are so big they won't fit into the 1,000 feet of usable length.

In 1939 a third set of locks was authorized and work started on them. They were to be much larger than the existing ones and, to make them less vulnerable to attack, were to be much stronger and located some distance away from the present locks. When the war started in 1941, the project was abandoned and never started again.

The dream of de Lesseps for a sea-level canal is today most seriously considered. Its backers say it would be much more difficult to put out of commission and even if bombed shut, need simply be dug out again. Such a canal could be used twenty-four hours a day and, as traffic increased, be widened indefinitely. The price tag for such a ditch would be gigantic, however, and dismays even its advocates.

Meanwhile all the old maps and surveys have been taken down out of the closet, dusted off and examined carefully. New surveying parties go out, return, and still others head into the wilds for additional mapping. Nicaragua, Tehuantepec, the Atrato River and all the others—all the old familiar names and places once again occupy the minds of canal builders. Nobody knows exactly what should be done, or how. They only agree that something must be done and quickly!

Soon, somewhere, a new generation of Tropical Tramps must shoulder their instruments and head into the bush. A site will have to be picked out. After them will follow the shovel men, the dynamiters, the concrete experts, the hydraulic engineers, the drillers, carpenters, plumbers, locomotive engineers, truck drivers, Diesel mechanics, bookkeepers . . . and no doubt, the brides!

The route to Cathay has gotten too big for its boots. It is coming apart at the seams. A new dream will have to be brought to reality. Uncle Sam peers southward a little anxiously. Those who live in Latin America gaze up at *Yanquilandia* also a bit uneasily. They both wonder where, and how soon.

For Further Reading

Abbott, Willis J. *Panama and The Canal*. New York: Syndicate Publishing Co., 1913.

Biesanz, John and Mavis. *The People of Panama*. New York: Columbia University Press, 1955.

Fast, Howard. *Goethals and The Panama Canal*. New York: Julian Messner, Inc., 1942.

Lee, Storrs. *Strength to Move a Mountain*. New York: G. P. Putnam's Sons. 1958.

Lindsay, John. *Panama and The Canal Today*. Boston: L. C. Page, 1910.

Nicolay, Helen. *Bridge of Water*. New York: Appleton-Century-Crofts, 1940.

The Panama Canal—25th Anniversary. Mt. Hope, Panama Canal Zone: Panama Canal Press, 1939.

Peck, Anne. *Pageant of Middle American History*. New York: Longmans Green & Co., 1947.

Siegfried, Andre. *Suez and Panama*. New York: Harcourt, Brace & Co., 1940.

Index

About the Author

PAUL RINK is a native Californian, born in San Jose on January 6, 1912 and now living in Monterey with his wife and two children. He majored in literature and science in college; has been an engineering officer in the Merchant Marine and on other ships. He lived in Panama for seven years where he engaged in the import-export business; was an engineer for the Panama Canal; served in the U. S. Embassy. During all the years of work, travel and study, Mr. Rink wrote continually, and his articles have appeared in national magazines. He has also worked in the documentary and semi-documentary field in TV and is the author of several books for young people.